JOYFUL LEARNING

No One Ever Wants to Go to Recess!

Gail Small

SCARECROWEDUCATION
Lanham, Maryland • Toronto • Oxford
2003

Published in the United States of America
by ScarecrowEducation
An imprint of The Rowman & Littlefield Publishing Group, Inc.
4501 Forbes Boulevard, Suite 200, Lanham, Maryland 20706
www.scaroweducation.com

PO Box 317
Oxford
OX2 9RU, UK

British Library Cataloguing in Publication Information Available

Library of Congress Cataloging-in-Publication Data

Small, Gail, 1947–
  Joyful learning : no one ever wants to go to recess! / Gail Small.
    p. cm.
  "A ScarecrowEducation Book."
  ISBN 0-8108-4743-4 (pbk. : alk. paper)
  1. Motivation in education. 2. Classroom environment. I. Title.
LB1065.S564 2003
370.15'4—dc21   2003000836

♾™ The paper used in this publication meets the minimum requirements of
American National Standard for Information Sciences—Permanence of Paper
for Printed Library Materials, ANSI/NISO Z39.48-1992.
Manufactured in the United States of America.

CONTENTS

DEDICATION

This book is dedicated to my "kids" of my thirty-three-year career. They have taught me so much, and without them, I'd have nothing to write about.

Once on a cruise in the middle of the ocean, traveling with a childhood friend who is now a teacher and psychologist, I was asked the question that supposedly everyone always wanted to ask: "What was your family really like?" I admit, it was an "Ozzie and Harriet" family, and not until later years did I appreciate my upbringing. To mom (my best friend), my brother Hal, and his wife Sue: There are no words to express my genuine love and appreciation.

To my son, Michael, for his courage, love, and especially our friendship.

To my late dad, who shared my dreams and taught me to find the positives in the multitude of experiences I continue to encounter daily.

To my many special friends, the families representing thirty-three years of teaching, and to you, the readers: It is with hope that you will look for the positives that can be found in all that you do.

ACKNOWLEDGMENTS

I truly appreciate each and every child who has become a part of me while teaching for thirty-three years. (Thank you to the parents for sharing your children with me!) Your support and energy has been phenomenal, and together you are *all* my extended family.

People somehow just come into my life, often unexpectedly. Because of you, my life is filled with excitement and enthusiasm. No two days are ever the same. Maybe that is why my passion for teaching is still the same (maybe more) than the first day I ever walked into my own classroom. I think something is "the best" and before I know it another "best" is happening.

Special thanks to:

Dr. Bill Glasser and Carleen: Your sharing—have I told you how much I appreciate you?

Dr. Brenda: Our talks/thoughts get me to higher places.

Bette: Your laughs and our love of elephants.

Bernie: I only went to sail and you taught me to soar.

Chris, Deva, Irv, Jan, Judy, Adrienne, Cathie, and Susie: Your continuous smiles and encouragement.

Cynthia: Since we were eight years old, your curiosity has always been catchy and fun.

Frank and Steve: You saved me on days when the computer would not cooperate.

Jackie: We met in first grade and our bond is so special.

Kim: You add dimension . . . we are two peas in a pod.

LuNel: For sharing our philosophies and moving *to make the difference!*

Ms. Colleen, Jennifer, Kylie, Lori, Lorraine, Sherry: You are the best!

Mrs. Barbara Romey: You define friendship.

Toni: We met by "accident" and I'm sure glad we did!

Zsa, Karen, Szilard: Pictures tell so much because of you.

Exceptional principals who truly believe in the best for the children and supported my creativity: Mr. Harold Howarth, the late Mr. William Jouvenat, Mr. Bernie Carr, Mrs. Marilyn Bayles, Mr. Larry Birdsell, Dr. Kristi White, and Mrs. Leean Nemeroff.

With much appreciation to student illustrators and contributors:

Adrian, Amina, Brigette, Cathy, Charlene, Clara, Conner, Courtney, Erica, Hailey, Heather, Irene, Jade, Jake, Jennifer, Jesse, Jessica, John, Kendra, Laura, Mai, Marley, Melissa, Micaela, Miriam, Shayna, Sky, Steven, and Jeffrey Mihaly.

Thank you to *everyone* I know (and even those I've yet to meet) for my extraordinary, everyday experiences.

FOREWORDS

It is my belief that a Choice Theory environment not only connects parents, students, and teachers but it is the basis for building a solid foundation for the development of character. The habits of caring, listening, supporting, contributing, encouraging, trusting, and befriending, build relationships and success. When there is no external control, students become interested in expressing themselves because they know someone cares for them and they have a say. I have visited with Ms. Small and her students where I have seen everyone totally engaged in the joy of learning. They are all working together and bringing out the best in each other. I can see why no one wants to go to recess. This book is a guide that will encourage and inspire all teachers to look forward to the next day with their students. This is learning at it's best.

—Dr. William Glasser

We've all moved through bookstores, self-help websites, and seminars by distinguished speakers to discover the mystery of reaching our children. The abundance of information can be overwhelming. But this collection of real-life experiences is a guide to build tools that jump-start the connection with each child you come into contact with. The keys to success are here, in these words, to stimulate ideas that can be adapted to anyone and will remain in readers' minds long after.

Gail has implemented encouragement with creativity for parents who are, first and foremost, teachers of their children. Her attitude—more a "discover it all" than "know it all"—draws everyone into a world of personal discovery. This helps parents bridge the gap between true achievable success and bland, boring book knowledge. This type of knowledge cuts across from educator to parental instinct with enlightenment: the idea of parents and teachers working as bookends to support our students, not to pressure and squeeze them.

Gail helps to open up everyone's sense of creativity and helps them to discover the inner passion and excellence that have gone unnoticed. Honoring each person's individuality is one of her keys to unlocking a student's gift. These newly discovered gifts will open a new world for the student, the teacher, the parent, and the entire family. Gail recognizes that parents bring intriguing perspectives to the curriculum and welcomes the newness that can be applied for the students. This overwhelming acceptance is felt and appreciated by each parent entering her classroom because, before long, each child will have excelled in areas never dreamed, reached goals seen as a far-off fantasy, and put forth and solidified the stick-to-itiveness for their future to blaze in understanding.

—Mrs. Kim Hersh (involved parent for over eight years)

INTRODUCTION

The experiences we bring to our students have an effect on their lives, the lives of their families, communities, country, and in fact, the entire world. Education is like tossing a pebble into the water: we realize that with the sound, there comes a rippling effect that each circle carries with it, and broadens out in an everlasting pattern of possibilities.

Children need a comfortable environment and a chance to progress to reach their potential. Young children enter their very first day of school with such genuine excitement and anticipation. My goal is to help readers realize the importance of this spirit and to keep it alive, while at the same time laying the foundation for each child's education and future. By involving the students, they become motivated. In a positive learning climate, students build the necessary tools and skills to better reach their total learning competency.

Imagine you are a student in a classroom where you are happy being you. You feel like your opinions matter, and you have a say in what you learn and how you learn it. Learning should be a fun and interesting adventure. Now imagine being a teacher in that classroom filled with students longing for knowledge. Picture being a parent welcomed into that classroom. The school atmosphere must be a place where children, parents, and teachers are encouraged to collaborate, thrive, share, celebrate and be the best they can be.

I *still* love each and every day. No two moments are *ever* the same. Each and every child is so unique and special! They are like sponges, ready to absorb as much as we will teach them. I would like to share my continued excitement and exuberance with new teachers, seasoned teachers, counselors, parents, and of course, the children!

1

LET THE REAL YOU SHINE OUT!

In teaching, personal adventures, interests, humor, stories, and experiences make learning come alive. When a teacher connects with the students, you catch the students' curiosity and desire. In any curriculum, no matter how academically based, you can weave in a little of yourself. Students long to retell your personal stories, retain your funny jingles or comparisons, become more interested, and  *want to learn more. Don't hesitate to share! Open up to them! They will open up back to you threefold and you never know when it is going to happen. Share your ideas, dreams, mistakes, and experiences. Enhance their knowledge and help them learn to enjoy/pursue life.*

Bubbles are universal. They have an aura, color, brilliance, and flow. A jar of bubbles, tucked away in a cupboard, can be reached for on any given day. As an icebreaker for any child (or adult), to motivate a lull in activities, to incorporate student reaction and involvement, bubbles can always create conversation and a smile. They can inspire written language, art, approximate measurement of size or distance traveled, and scientific discoveries. It is also fun to mix bubble solutions and have all the students release bubbles into the air at the same time. Sometimes after a major student (class/school) accomplishment, blowing bubbles is a visual way to commemorate success.

I take bubbles when I travel. As a ship sails or a band plays, bubbles can add sparkle to any event, anywhere. I was leaving the island of St. Maarten at the end of a sailing adventure and I still had some bubble solution. Rather than toss it out as the

Jasmine Manoukian

taxi was about to take me to the airport, I asked the driver to stop. I ran and gave my bubbles to strangers sitting at an outdoor café near the water. I could hear their different languages and I handed the bubbles to some people—total strangers—without a word. As the taxi pulled away, I looked out the rearview window and I could see strangers interacting with a sudden loud chatter. The people blended together and began blowing bubbles. Bubbles were floating into the air and total strangers were yelling "thank you" (I think!) in different languages as they all waved to me. My sadness at leaving the island dissolved.

POLISH

Dr. Connie Holliman believes:

> A happy classroom is like a used car lot. Each car or student comes onto the lot from different owners and with different experiences. The owner or teacher helps each car or student by polishing and fine-tuning so that it can function at its best. This is done by spending time with each car or student to evaluate the needs that need to be met and strengths to build on to prepare each car or student to leave the lot or classroom. The time spent on the relationship determines the perceived value of the car or student. (Holliman 2002)

WHEN YOU SHINE, THEY REFLECT!

Words of a former student, Jane Dmochowski:

I consider myself a successful woman. I am completing my Ph.D. in geophysics and am teaching geology at a community college. When I graduated from college, I was nominated valedictorian by the faculty and deans of my university. My mother, feeling extremely proud of her youngest daughter, sent copies of a newspaper article written about me to nearly everyone she knew. There was one person, however, that got a thank-you letter instead. That person was Gail Small, an elementary school teacher of mine. My mom realized, as I do now, that some people shouldn't be informed of my success—some should be congratulated. Gail helped to build my self-esteem so that I could be successful.

Things do not come easily to everyone, but it doesn't mean those things will never come. At the beginning of elementary school, I struggled with reading, was quiet, and was not considered particularly smart. Somehow, by the end of Ms. Gail's class, I knew I was smart and nobody could tell me otherwise. From that moment, there was no stopping me. I remember feeling like a full human being in Gail's class. I was no longer just a little kid with cute blonde ponytails. Everyone was important! I strongly believe that the importance of individuality and pride in oneself taught by Gail contributed to my success in and out of school.

I am thankful for those who touched my life. But I am particularly indebted to those, like Gail Small, who paid special attention to my individual talents and needs to ensure that I was taught in the most effective and the most fun way possible. These are the people to whom I owe my love of learning.

Jane Heineman in third grade.

Jane Dmochowski at CalTech.

The special touches—like immense and special praise for a job well done; circle time for individual needs, worries, and joys to be shared; and the time spent to really know each student (and in many cases the children's families as well)—are what set one teacher apart from others. Ms. Small went beyond the traditional curriculum in order to pique every child's interest.

She even got my family to host a German exchange student by convincing my mother that it would be a learning experience for her children. Indeed it was! That experience incited my interest in the German language and international travel so much that I studied German for four years in high school and have traveled extensively since graduating from college. Simply put, the creativity Gail employs in teaching children has had an invaluable influence on my life. My hope is that others who have the potential and the opportunity to teach young lives may learn from this wisdom, enthusiasm, and experience.

2

COMMUNICATION

In everything *you do,* communicate clearly! *I suggest that when
elementary-aged children bring
anything from home, be sure the
object selected is appropriate and
approved by the parents. (Maybe
include this in your class "rules"
. . . or you might have to learn
the hard way, as I did.)*

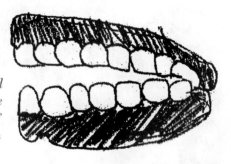

One day I asked a first grade class, "Tomorrow each bring something special and different." (Seemed easy enough.) We were at a dictation level, with transition actually going into the development of prewriting skills. They would show the object, and every child would illustrate, dictate, or write about it, depending on his or her individual level.

What a great lesson I thought I had designed as I began the process with such zest. We even waited until the afternoon, building up the excitement and curiosity of all. It was going so well—could it be a model lesson? Maybe? Not! Their animated faces were darling as they shared using vivid, descriptive words to illustrate the special animal, their treasures. First was G.I. Joe, then a doll, favorite stu shells from the ocean, an athletic team hat, and—Great-Grandma's false teeth! A child was lucky enough to have Great-Grandma visiting from out of state. That child's family even got to share all of the excitement and curiosity of my lesson in communication because they were dialoguing with every adult in the family and with nearby neighbors as well.

Unfortunately, they were not lucky enough to have any clue of where aging Great-Grandma had put her false teeth. The family was beside itself turning the entire house upside down. They even wondered if Alzheimer's had crept in overnight. My popularity as a teacher definitely soared that day when I called to tell the family I had Great-Grandma's false teeth!

AND . . . THEY TAKE YOU LITERALLY!

Children take us word for word, I know that, yet only recently in the middle of a messy project, with all hands gooey and full of paint and glue, I said, "Hands up." What I meant was to get their hands off of their finished projects to best maintain their wonderful creations. Instead of the hands lifting off the works in progress, into the air went all hands *up*! The drips and mess gave us all a start, until we looked at each other and couldn't help but laugh. Watch when you give explicit directions! I gave instructions for the first spelling test: "Name, date, put the numbers one to ten." As I walked around to begin giving the words, the first paper I noticed said "one to ten."

One day a child started crying, sobbing in class. (This was twenty-plus years ago, but I remember it as if it happened yesterday.) We were ready to go to lunch on what seemed a normal school day. He was too upset to verbalize and shook his head, refusing to eat or play. What was going on in this young boy's life? Why was he so sensitive and unapproachable? I, the teacher, along with the school nurse, counselor, and principal, were completely baffled and tried to decipher the problem. This child had come from another school and was overcoming social problems and loopholes in his educational development. He was finally happy and making great strides. He was just beginning to have friends and could actually feel his daily progress. Such a simple thing, when we finally were to understand. That night was Open House! Little Bobby thought the school was being sold and he would have to leave his new friends and familiar surroundings.

One morning after I took the attendance, I set the folder down on a table. When I realized what I had forgotten, I asked Melissa, a cute second grader standing near me, to "Please hurry and hop the attendance folder to the office." As I began my lesson, knowing she would be right back, a colleague came in and said, "Do you know that you have a child hopping through the school?" I felt puzzled and had no idea what she was talking about. When I did, and Melissa returned to class, together we got out dictionaries and learned about the word "literal." No, no one laughed at her. I made it clear to the class that it was I who needed "help." Since that day, I encourage everyone to remember to express oneself with the exact words that one wants others to hear. Children (and parents) must be able to interpret your assignments, directions, and comments.

Jesse

He was a struggling reader, English was a new language, and his fluency in reading was very minimal. I always tell the students to read orally and talk into a tape recorder so they can hear their words out loud. Also, with a laugh I say, "Read to your family, the dog, the wall, a bird, just read out loud!" As time went by, this little guy became more proficient in oral reading. It seemed easier for him and he was more relaxed. When I praised him and asked his family what he was doing differently, the laugh was on me. He was reading every night—to the family bird! We are now waiting to hear if the cockatiel has developed better verbal communication skills, too!

Through development, confidence, and direction, the natural flow of language comes about. Children learning how to get along with each other are developing personal and social awareness. They hear words, sounds, inflections, and the rhythm of language. Proficiency includes combining multiple skills to converse, express, and *communicate*. Encourage students to exchange/accept each other's words, thoughts, and ideas. Teaching communication includes many components that affect understanding in everyday life as well as academic performance.

Take some time to include some simple exercises that in the end will take your class to higher levels of thinking. Communication includes many forms: drawn, oral, written, or even photographed. All forms of communication lead to listening, seeing, and understanding. A twist or variation of a lesson, especially in the beginning of a school year, will cultivate student listening, contribution, and involvement in any subject matter. Every teacher/every lesson needs questions, answers, discussions, exploration, observation and interpretation. Academic details will expand if students are comfortable and ready to receive all that you can teach them. Realistically, when young children develop the capacity to better think and express on their own, they can apply these skills to all subject matters throughout their education and everyday life experiences.

FAVORITE EXERCISES THAT ELICIT COMMUNICATION

Sounds: Make a tape recording of interesting sounds. Students can illustrate or write about what they are hearing. The unknown can be tricky and elicit descriptive stories and poetry. Assign a student (or group) to tape varied sounds and lead the class in communicative responses with substantial, supportive reasoning.

Variation Sound Lesson: You hear a dog barking in the next room (but there are no dogs there). Imagine your surprise when you find it is only a tape recording! Listening to sounds can make life more interesting as your senses are aroused, for you can hear so many different sounds. Voices in an unknown language, birds chirping, cows mooing, music for dancing, laughter, even crying are all forms of communication. Discussion will be stimulating with many ideas about what was being communicated in all of the sounds.

Puppetry: Students have a chance to read and present without memorization or stage fright. Studying scripts includes repetition that builds confidence. Puppeteers become cooperative and flexible in the close quarters behind a puppet stage. Be sure to peek behind the scenes! You will see true collaboration as puppets appear on stage. Children learn patience as they give each other cues. Together they share the sounds of audience laughter and approval.

To quote noted speech pathologist Del Hultgren: "Puppetry is nonthreatening to children. They can go into the world of fantasy and make up their own stories or they can retell stories where they tap into the following skills—memory, sequencing, vocabulary, meaning through intonation and finally the love of storytelling and knowing our national heritage through the old faithful fairy tales and nursery rhymes" (Hultgren 2002).

Behind the scenes of a puppet theatre.

Sign Language: A unique means of communication. For the hearing impaired, this is a means of communication most often used, although there are variations in sign language just as there are dialects in spoken languages. Your students can share or write poetry and music, and put "words" into sign language. This takes the lesson to another dimension and introduces children to what it is when they see people signing. (It's also great as a presentation for a holiday or special show.)

Photography: Photography captivates and inspires. Images viewed are communicated with artistic expression and meaning. Photos can be identified and bring about stories, nostalgia, and a wealth of information. Have students bring photos and create a collage. (individually, in groups, or as a class) Pictures can be of or about your students or a topic relating to the current curriculum. Obtain disposable cameras and use these to not only photograph but to ignite discussion and interpretation. Foster new interest in the scientific process. For example, one could document the chronological growth of a seedling, changing weather, or the sequence of a story. Students taking the same picture can have a different angle or perspective with varied results and descriptions. Photography can heighten any topic and be a powerful tool in a variety of academic studies.

Comparison Activity: Reinforce terminology and emphasize concepts that you are teaching. Place two boxes side by side. In each box, place a similar object, picture, or word. Participants must evaluate the likes and differences of the relevant subject matter (World War I and World War

II, odd numbers and even numbers, and so forth). Communication can be oral through group discussion or nongraded competition. Communication can be written (individually or in teams) to define differences and definition.

Place a word relevant to your immediate academic study on a student's head for others to view. (Use a bobby pin, headband, or anything—just be sure he or she doesn't see what it says.) Establish rules for contributing so classmates give clear and significant clues to elicit appropriate guesses. This is great for vocabulary words, scientific terminology, or even words taken from map legends. It is an appropriate skill review and students are using their words to explain the definitions that you strive for them to master. (Try it with math facts—different ways to get the same answer.) While this interaction encourages thinking and factual answers, students are eager to participate in your academic "review."

Dr. Shanté Morgan, professor of communications, states "You have to be a good listener in order to communicate well" (Morgan 2003). When students tell you that they *always* listen, try this: (The older the student, the better.) Have a pair of students sit back to back so they can't see what is in the other's hands. Give them each a baggie with the same contents. You can use props of blocks, buttons, feathers, or varied materials. My favorite is toothpicks, pliable gumdrop candy (different sizes and kinds), and marshmallows (small and large). They will each have an opportunity to give thorough verbal directions to their partner as they create some type of object with the contents of the baggie. (No peeking!) The other student follows the exact directions and attempts to position each of the materials as directed. (If you don't choose to use "materials," you can use pencil and paper to draw or describe it in writing.) This "experiment" is astounding to watch when they turn around to see if their creations are exact. Ninety percent of the time, they do not match exactly! This opens students' eyes to the fact that truly being "on task" does make a difference, and the importance of "listening to the teacher!"

COMMUNICATION WITHOUT COMMON LANGUAGE

When children learn to feel good about themselves, they begin to have the capacity to reach out to others. Body language is a form of communication. When a total stranger arrives, speaking a foreign language that no one can begin to converse in, the natural warmth of children truly makes a difference.

One day, a seven-year-old Norwegian girl stood in the school office with her mom hoping for a place in our school. She spoke no English and the mother stated that she needed to be in the classroom with her daughter because they had just arrived from Norway and her child was petrified. The school year was well under way and class enrollments were full. Sometimes something like this is not a problem, but an opportunity! When we open to new experiences, there are also new possibilities. I asked her to join our class and as we embraced her culture; she not only developed, but so did every child in the class. Her face showed fear and curiosity, yet there was a little twinkle in her eyes. She listened and observed, the children listened and watched, while also sharing and exchanging welcoming smiles and words. At the end of the first day, Amina proudly went home to tell all that she had already learned some English. I tend to say "Excuse me" when giving children another chance to redirect their focus, work, or behavior. Amina's first English was "Excuse me." Out of context, yes, yet mastery of her first words to begin to communicate in a new and challenging language and environment.

Day by day, Amina's confidence developed as she grasped our language and way of life. The children learned about another culture as maps appeared, along with Scandinavian music. Cooking traditional foods was fascinating and yummy. Communication began to flow through interest and special interaction. She came a long way and so did everyone who had the privilege of this experience. No one will forget the day she *finally* began to speak English in complete sentences and was verbalizing loudly in the girls' bathroom, not knowing it backed up to a class in session. An adult reprimanded her about her outburst, having no idea she spoke limited English. Amina came back to class in tears, not comprehending what was screamed at her. Educators need to communicate and be sensitive with each child and every situation.

We also cannot forget the day when Amina gained enough self-esteem and went to the front of the classroom with a confident look on her face! Using English, to explain her alphabet sounds, blends, and vowels, she wrote on the board extending to us a way to develop some "bilingual" vocabulary. Unexpectedly, she had to return to her home country but the memory of Amina will always be a part of every member of that class. Our last interaction was the children asking if we could all sit in a circle and talk to or with Amina. Young students shared with Amina and each other that because of her they now knew more about communication as well as about places faraway in the world, that we all *really* are alike, as well as different. As children exchanged their thoughts and ideas, parents walked in and could only listen to the lessons their children had absorbed, way beyond any books we had ever studied. As all turned to me for guidance, my tears flowing and speechless, I reached for a tape to record this day for Amina. She took with her plentiful lessons and newly acquired knowledge. She also took the tape with the voices of her American friends who had taught her so much. Though the good-byes were tearful and emotional, the memories are treasured.

Years later, I received the following e-mail from Amina:

I remember I was first scared and felt lost, as if I was alone in the whole world. It started out classmates wanted to play with me and were curious. Me and the other kids used the body language to understand each other. Also, fingers and hands, faces, whatever we could use to . . . talk. It sometimes made me angry when I couldn't understand what people laughed about or were learning. Sometimes I didn't have a clue what to do or say. Yet, a new world opened up for me. Winter is almost here now and it is cold and freezing. It seems like rain has no ending . . . it is in days like this we really miss "Amerika."

Amina enters school in the U.S.A.

MULTIRACIAL THOUGHTS

Communication is a means to face and express some of the problems in our society today. Sadly, some young children feel and experience discrimination. One student, in a conversation at home with her family, talked of never having any African American friends. As Holly chattered on, her parents listened and later told me this story. You see, this child's best friend is of a racial mixture. Because I strive for children accepting people for who they are, this beautiful and sincere statement was meaningful to all of us.

One of my former students, Desiree, reflected back on elementary school:

Desiree Perkins in second grade.

Desiree as a teen.

Lots of people made me feel *uncomfortable*. I'd try to be friendly and play with them. Then, they would just reject me. I would go away to any corner and just start to cry. So one day we all talked about it in circle. No one realized before how I felt inside. People tried to understand how it was "to be different" and tried harder. Then I finally started to make friends. Now that we're grown, I hope they always think twice about anyone they might meet in the future. Words and actions are far more valuable than jewels. If I didn't begin to communicate, I might always be in a corner.

Her family, Michael Blade, Romaine Mazer, and Susan Perkins, shared these words:

Others need to become aware of your style of educating our new generation and hopefully more teachers will take up the path you have so unerringly begun. At a young age, Desiree already had a full plate. Being of mixed background; African American and white, her parents divorced, another woman in her life to help guide her, bouncing back and forth between two households . . . she was insecure and confused.

Your classroom was a safe haven where she learned to communicate. A place where she could express her anger, ask questions and get answers, and be guided into making choices that will benefit her for her lifetime. She felt secure and accepted. She began to view her "differences" as something that made her special. We saw her grow from a shy child into a bright, curious, confident young lady.

As a father, it gave me particular joy to perform my music for the children. Bringing musician friends to give a concert using African rhythm instruments added to the other children's knowledge while broadening their outlook. Your dedication to growing children in a positive and creative way will always be remembered and appreciated by all of her "parents" and the people whose lives she will touch in her surely bright future.

MATHEMATICAL COMMUNICATION

As the language of mathematics becomes natural, students develop symbols, operations, and vocabulary. Expose children to experiences so they can gather evidence to build, support, and explain their reasoning. Students need to communicate with reasons supporting investigations and open-ended problems. Mathematics (and science) should be appropriately integrated with all academics. Communication includes expression, explanation, and the support for strategies in all subject matter within and outside of school.

FROM A CHILD'S POINT OF VIEW

While young, Randy's parents volunteered and she participated in activities as she got to know me during the years that her big brother was in my class. She waited for her turn and assumed she would be in my class too. With the numbers and class configurations, she was not placed in my class but one day a letter appeared from Randy: "Dear Ms. Gal, Today I'm really happy I get to viset you. I'd really like to be in your class some day caus I neve ben in your class befor. I think I've been in Ms. H's class anof and it duset mean that I don't like her! Caus sometimes I have to go somewhar else. Love, Randy."

Obviously, this was an independent idea all her own, and for a young child, she conveyed her thoughts. Sometimes the potential of a child is intriguing. In her disappointment, she stated her concerns, reasons, and frustrations. No, we don't let children dictate to us, but it was so thought out and expressive that we both talked with Randy and changed her class. This is an example of a child openly expressing her thoughts. If every child could feel secure enough to talk to his or her teachers and parents, what a wonderful system (future) this could be!

COMMUNICATORS

"What did you do in school today?" How many of us have been asked that while growing up? Who has asked his or her own child this question? And, amazingly so, the answer is—"Nothing!"

A "communicator" is a log (separate from a journal) that is written daily. It begins with the five-year-old who draws a mere picture and a date on the paper. This gradually evolves into a sentence. The older students might start with one or two sentences that later develop into paragraphs. Whatever the level, the purpose of the communicator is to further develop the communication between children and parents.

Children can write what happened during the day at school or if something special is happening tomorrow. They can share questions, significant moments, or lessons learned. Written skills begin to share personal thoughts, feelings, hopes, and disappointments. The technique of writing is a healthy means of communication. Many families have revealed that this informative method has opened up new doors for parent and child communication. ("Dinner-table discussions have especially become more fluid and meaningful.) Even the "too-busy parent" begins to read the words and better understand more about his or her own child. The communicator can be read with ease and is to be initialed daily by parents. Often they write a question or comment back to their child or even the teacher, as necessary. The daily communication back and forth between child and parents is something that many begin to look forward to.

I check this communicator weekly and write a teacher response. No matter how much time a teacher gives to each student, there are so many little things left unknown. The communicator gives more insight into each child's inner thoughts, feelings, and curiosities. Being better informed, helps me to be a better teacher. Some things that often go unanswered are addressed through the tool of written communication. The students identify more with the teacher who reads the little personal comments, reactions, and suggestions on a regular basis. What a keepsake, when summer quickly arrives—a daily commentary on everything experienced during the entire school year!

WRITTEN COMMUNICATION

Oral language flows naturally into reading and written expression. Students can illustrate, dictate, write, read, and compile many original selections. You can supply ideas, story starters, and experiences so that this entire process can begin to unfold. A simply motivated topic can develop into a world of writing and reading.

Every student has a message that he or she can (and needs) to share! The child who is learning to communicate is actively involved in a process. Language is the way people share their thinking and we want our students to develop effective language skills. Fluency develops through experience and that is why oral and written language and communication are important in our everyday teaching. This encompasses children sharing their thoughts, receptive listening, and expressive, meaningful communication.

TRUE COMMUNICATION

Dr. Helen McIntosh explains:

> Everyone needs a place to go for comfort/resolution . . . to openly express, dialogue, and connect. If we really want a zero tolerance for violence in our schools, then we have to have a zero tolerance for any form of disrespect. Disrespect is the non-physical form of violence, but will lead to more physical forms of violence if ignored. Building character, you will develop a place where words are expressed so that healthy relationships can thrive. (McIntosh 1999)

As you, the teacher, instill confidence in your students and make them feel comfortable, they will give more attention to their work and to each other. When you truly communicate as an educator, you are better able to keep alive your "vision" about why you started teaching in the first place. Teacher self-esteem escalates when there is a high level of give and take exchange. "Expression" and interaction stimulate involvement, which transforms and ignites your every lesson and goal.

I believe that you *never* know what to expect in teaching. One day, an unexpected occurrence confirmed my belief in the written language and the importance of establishing and teaching communication. I was teaching a morning lesson when an eight-year-old student of mine came in late and handed me a note. I just figured (wrong) that it was a tardy note and went about what we were doing. Until I looked at her face, and then I read her note . . . five times! "Please give me extra attention to-day. I watched daddy hit mommy and the police all came too."

Though this family fell upside down, as years went by, the child's life eventually normalized. Because parent and teacher communication is so important, in time "Daddy" sent me this note: "A world of thanks to you. Thank you for your steadfast belief and encouragement. You have been a fantastic gardener of the flowers of our future, our children."

③

MOTIVATION

Sitting in a concert hall, I could feel the emotion of the music as I watched the pianist's fingers dance on the keys of the piano. As my body felt the rhythm and I listened to the melody, I became part of the crowd's enthusiastic approval. I marveled at the talent of the young man who was sitting at the keyboard and my mind flashed back to 1969 when he was my student.

Sometimes motivation doesn't come to fruition for years and then one day you discover a previous student's life was affected by an event that occurred in your classroom.

My very first year of teaching, I placed a toy wooden piano in my classroom. Every day, as my students entered in and out of the room, I encouraged them to express themselves on this instrument. Some were intrigued by the sounds they could make, while others were more interested in watching how the sounds were produced inside the piano. Eventually, even I was tired of the improvisational noise. (Music?) One day, I put the piano outside and said, "Anyone who wants this toy piano, take it!"

Twenty some years later, I began getting phone messages from someone named Bradley. Of course, I was curious as to who or what this was all about. Teaching is full of surprises! The student who had relieved me of that toy piano was being featured as the fine musician from the world-famous San Francisco Music Conservatory. So with flowers, my mother, pride and genuine warmth deep inside me, I attended his concert. He smiled and as he went on stage, Brad told me, "I still remember all of the positive things you did. I have so many memories that you gave me."

When you teach music, you incorporate the mathematical qualities of patterns, notes, and rhythms. Helping students understand composers teaches them to recognize different styles, moods, and talents. While compiling this book, Brad's parents surprised me with my words of encouragement that I had written to Brad thirty years ago:

Motivation is turning people on to looking at things in a new way. When you create an environment that heightens intrigue and curiosity, students respond and want to seek answers. I see students learning while discovering. I strive to involve them and capture their interests. In education, there are no neutral moments because everything you do as an educator affects the children. Making a child feel good will motivate him or her but making one unhappy will shut down a child. Neither a student nor the teacher will get anywhere if you just "let them be." Motivation is the circumstance of the existing and changing learning environment. Exposing children to new objects, thoughts, and experiences influences and motivates them.

Inspiring children to discover learning brings imagination into education.

MOTIVATIONAL GAMES

Games can be designed for students to have fun while learning. Concepts can be introduced in which students experience increased interest

and success. Games can be made for any and every academic study. This is also an appropriate homework assignment to stimulate individuals or small groups. Take vocabulary words and randomly arrange them on a board. Add a free space, lose a turn, go forward five spaces, or something to add interest while playing. Try putting math facts, history dates, or state capitals in spaces Add a spinner, buttons, or "lost" tops from felt-tip pens to improvise as playing pieces to move about the gameboard as skills soar. It is interesting to guide students to figure the proportions for a three-dimensional figure as you make dice for your games. It is rewarding for students to write appropriate questions on cards that can be stacked and drawn as part of the game playing process.

Challenge, choice, and strategy are a part of the game experience that improves and reinforces skills. Games can be for individuals, small groups, or a whole class. Learning through games can change a child's attitude and empower a child to build skills while exploring concepts. I find that reasoning and problem solving elevate because of the incentive when the "facts" are played in fun. Children think, formulate questions, and exchange ideas in meaningful conversation. They also learn from each other as well as from their differences. Children may focus on a relevant concept as they unconsciously and successfully achieve mastery while playing "games."

Games can be educational exercises for independent workers to accelerate skills while peers are engaged in other group or classroom lessons (or challenging when work is complete). "Game" material corresponds to daily learning concepts. Some students learn better from a game instead of a routine workbook or exercise. At times, obstacles can be overcome through varied educational practices. A means of evaluation can be the mastery of a concept focused on in a given game. Games are a valuable tool to "reteach" and employ strategies and understanding. The excitement of games carries enthusiasm into the entire learning process! Students are thinking and begin seeking more challenge. The effectiveness of the game experience not only extends and measures change and growth in academic skills, but it also is enjoyable.

Terri Nelson explains how games motivated her:

At five years old, I think I was one of the luckiest children around to find that school was not the grim boring place most children dread, but instead was a place of wonder, of enlightenment, and most of all . . . fun. I attribute that to a very special teacher who brought learning to life in a way that made children want to know more. You were enjoying the process so much you didn't even realize you were (gasp) *learning*. One of my favorite parts of class was game time. After all, what child doesn't love to get to play games, especially when you're getting to play instead of having to do boring schoolwork and memorizing? What I didn't realize was that these were very special games developed by our teacher. Each was a learning tool, a way to internalize the fundamentals we were taught. Each of the games was different, some involved math, others vocabulary, all were challenging and fun. It was a privilege to play the games. How many teachers have children who go out of their way to be good just to get to learn more? That is how our class was set up—if you were good, you were allowed to play games. It is not surprising we had some of the best-behaved children in our class because we were rewarded for our efforts with more learning but in a fun setting that was relaxing and enjoyable.

Terri Miller in second grade (now Terri Nelson: Executive Finance Director for the Los Angeles Newspaper Group).

CENTERS

A center is a highly motivational area where learning activities are available for hands-on learning and discovery. Centers are enticing for students to learn in a positive and challenging experience. "Spell out" your directions so students can work independently or in cluster groups to achieve the skills presented. Centers can apply to every subject and should be rotated and available for ongoing effective learning. Centers are successful experiences that help students understand principles through a more visual or self-discovery approach. Accomplishing these tasks induces responsibility as well as a boost for student self-image!

Centers can be at a specific time for an entire class or children can be scheduled for designated centers or times. I have used centers with students of all ages and to implement every concept imaginable. If you have not used centers with your students, introduce only a few in the beginning. Success is best attained if you first clearly demonstrate how to solve multitask (at times open-ended) projects. Depending on your purpose and program, you might want to have a checklist for students to check off centers as they complete them. (Try color-coding subjects or specific skills as you feel necessary.) Make each center appealing so students will gravitate to them and include a label or sign to identify your objective.

Find a way to select the value of your centers. I focus on *not* using paper and pencil activities. Sometimes class discussion becomes a measure of the progress achieved. A skill might be part of a progression to support the next skill you are going to introduce. When students are familiar with the concept of centers, include their help in adjusting or originating exciting centers to reinforce your course of studies.

OBSOLETE

Someone dumped a huge box of torn and tattered obsolete books at my doorstep. I guess they were delivered because the giver figured if anyone knew what to do with them it was me! It was somewhat of a *mystery*. Maybe that is why the students couldn't wait to get their hands on them and devoured them with curiosity, producing new ideas. This acquisition included something way beyond the outward appearance of tattered and torn. Once examined, I (we) found intriguing books (beautiful to us) of poetry, photography, history, magic, geography, and even science experiments. It was just another day that no one wanted to go to recess. Silent and cooperative reading ensued. No, not a predetermined lesson, but sometimes you have to let your students be your guide.

Motivation steers students to discover abilities that they didn't even know existed. A whole new world opens up with uncharted avenues to follow and explore.

Schools help mold the lives of young people who come from all walks of life. Many students experience unhappiness, failure, pain, and struggling. A supportive, motivational school experience can mean enrichment for every child. A child with a deficient home or family life needs stronger motivation and more successful learning experiences. Different home and family environments can necessitate different goals, needs, expectations, and behavior. In *Schools without Failure*, Dr. William Glasser states that "regardless of how many failures a person has had in the past, regardless of his background, his culture, his color, or his economic level, he will not succeed in general until he can some way first experience success in one important part of his life" (Glasser 1969). Glasser also feels, "I believe that if a child, no matter what his background, can succeed in school, he has an excellent chance for success in life. Knowledge and the ability to think are required to achieve worthwhileness."

Motivated students find tangible solutions. It is what an educator does with the students that makes the learning effective. Positive reinforcement delivers a strong message and elicits stronger student interest and learning. It is like translating a foreign language! They not only need to hear the words being said (lessons presented) but understand, digest and apply the instruction.

Teaching should include the necessary strategies (fuel) to motivate learners to reach their maximization of learning. Ask yourself what variables will best influence and motivate your students to reach positive educational goals. When they are involved in the process, opportunities will give continuous definition to expand educational accomplishments. If children are continuously enriched, there isn't a barrier or a stopping point.

In reality, the prescribed academic requirements are achieved at different times and in different ways for each individual student. Remember—each one will assimilate your instruction in his or her own way. Learning styles vary and the learning process is affected by student interest and teacher motivation.

When we work with children we are an influential force in each child's life. Classroom aide Eileen Hokana gave her unconditional patience and understanding as she took the time to incorporate the positives and focus on nonstop learning. Always approachable to the students, she'd give encouragement, often tearing down existing negatives that some children came with. Discussing motivational techniques years later, she shared: "When I am asked what I do if a child refuses to work on an assignment, I reply that I try to make the task more fun. If a student doesn't understand an assignment or want to do it, represent it so that they will be successful. No two students learn the same. We need to listen *and* look for the good to bring out their *best*."

PROVIDE MANY WAYS TO LEARN

Develop a repertoire of useful techniques for effective fluency in learning. Guide students to maintain appropriate interest while exploring and progressing. I know there are district goals to meet, yet concentration and intellectual challenge will meet and exceed the standards. I suggest the following supplementary materials and activities as another application to accommodate the academic principles you want your students to identify and master:

- Hands-on learning activities
- Encouragement of invention/creation
- Group investigation—Possible research, project, survey, chart
- Varied texts—Teacher presenting stimulating related readings
- Homework—Give a choice of possibilities (same topic, yet student choice and alternatives)
- Drama—Writing plays or puppet shows (application of concrete facts while increasing writing skills)
- Journalism—Reporting achieved academic criteria
- Compose radio or video types of broadcasts
- A class board for posting of appropriate and interesting data to complement or enhance studies

As Heather Perkins was packing to leave for college, she describes how she felt:

> First grade was happiness, one of the best years I've had yet. I always keep a few key ideas in mind and that's the way you learn. No matter what I do in life I always try my hardest and put forth as much effort as I can. I think as long as there's a goal, and as long as you don't lose sight of that goal, you accomplish it. In my mind, you will always be the one who connected everything I did through reading and writing because that is what I loved. When one has a desire to learn as much as possible, there becomes an interest at every level. As long as you can find something you're good at, something that makes you happy, you can use that confidence in other parts of your life.

Puzzled about your presentation for student advancement and fulfilling in-depth components to reach mastery? My favorite solution is . . . a puzzle!

Give your students a blank piece of paper, a marker, and an envelope. Make a list for them or compile it with them, of words that are essential for mastery in your current course of study. The students may write the words anywhere they wish on the paper. When this is done, ask them to turn over the paper and cut it into random puzzle pieces. Next, they should place each of the puzzle parts in an envelope. This can be a novel homework assignment to review word recognition or to look up the definitions. By writing words, they begin to retain what they write. By putting the puzzle together, students see (and begin to "own") those words. Puzzles can also be assembled and played through small or large group clustering. You may adjust the words or tasks, as well as vary your assignments for multiple instructional needs or levels.

Puzzle Variation: Similarly, instead of creating puzzles, create bingo cards. Insert words, math concepts, or even foreign languages in the spaces on the cards. The location of the written concepts on the bingo cards will vary. Use beans (or whatever) for markers to cover the spaces. Students can share teamwork and excitement working together, a few on one card. You can also find this a lesson in following directions if you play corners, or specific rows or patterns. (For young children, this is ideal for number recognition.) Whether students play bingo in class or at home for homework, unconsciously they are successfully absorbing the skills you want them to focus on.

Transform "expected" lessons into inventive surprises. Keep your students guessing and eager to anticipate what or how you will teach next. Once a parent, seemingly confused, came to ask me "Why does my child say he plays in class?" I took that as a compliment, because his test scores went up along with his attitude and interest. He was continuously responding to as much as I could give him and truly receiving the dividends of varied instruction.

California Lutheran University observer Andrea Monden notes:

I can easily see how students can be motivated to take on anything that comes their way when supported by caring encouragement and direction that enhances their spirit and self-confidence. A few minutes spent with Gail and her "cuties" can enlighten any visitor to the structured vision and direction of the class. The curriculum and corresponding activities cultivate an incredible variety of learning opportunities for the students to experience. They all understand their responsibilities and take control of their individual orientations. Whenever I go to observe, the children are eager to show me assignments they have accomplished and even talk to me about other things they have going on. I have gotten to know several of them and enjoy watching them grow as they continue to reach their goals and look forward to hopes of the future.

SILENCE IN THE CLASSROOM

Walking into the room, there is not a sound and each student is doing his or her own individual work. *Silence*! Buy a bag containing wrapped lollipops of different colors. When students open the lollipops, they are to save the wrappers. These assemble into a great collage to look at and become a math lesson for the near future. Of course! Relevant data to graph the number of wrappers by color! Important data and sincere student involvement. This is important educational information! They will record their findings mathematically and write about them as well.

Students counting the licks is what kept them so silently enthralled in quiet learning. Tally by ones, remember to cross the tally at five. Count by tens, circle with a color to show groups of 100? 1000? Who has more? Less? Note their smiles and there is always something to look forward to. Do this again at a later date and compare all data.

Silence?! Not usual in my classroom! The rule is "talking" is allowed if I can't distinguish who is talking. There is a time for everything. Part of learning is communicating, though not to disturb others from learning. The dynamics of discussion is a facet of discovery and motivation.

HOW TO GIVE TO THE CHILDREN?

As an educator, you influence your students. Be dynamic! Make something happen! Raise the probability for your students to become curious by initiating something more than the expected! If they feel comfortable and aroused, success will be more probable. Intrinsic motivation is when learning itself is "the prize."

Allison Butler, once my student, says:

My early education was a life-changing experience. It is amazing that at such a young age I realized my creativity and intelligence, and that others noticed it as well. Children are so impressionable and it is only through great teaching combined with exciting activities that they enjoy learning. Every child should have this valuable experience. Once I realized my creativity, it opened so many doors for me to explore and learn. It helped me excel, not only in school but socially as well.

Allison Butler in first grade.

Allison Butler: UCLA student.

As you motivate children, you are illustrating and influencing a multitude of possibilities for them. Emphasize challenge, creativity, and encourage perseverance. Help them improve their ability to develop and incorporate ideas through questions, brainstorming, and strategies. Elicit and reinforce independence and interpretation as an extension of meaningful learning.

Dr. Shanté Morgan shares the following thought:

Motivation—I believe the problem many educators, teachers, and parents have in failing to motivate children to success is by placing them in a box. Each child is born with a different set of DNA that makes us unique and special individuals. We should honor and respect children's (peoples) differences and encourage them to shine in their own light. They will not all excel in athletics, math, science, and the arts, but *they have excelled when they have done their best*. It is our responsibility as teachers, educators, and parents to find those special qualities and give children the opportunity to soar. (Morgan 2002)

4

POSITIVE SELF-ESTEEM

*Every child can find an outlet
and feel success in his or her
own way!*

Imagine starting each
and every day in a posi-
tive way! It's easy to
guide children to think
in a positive mode. Include
your students in a mo-
ment of *your* thoughts at
the beginning of the day.
Whether it is a light misty rain that
you are enjoying or the fact that you heard a favorite song on the radio,
these are examples of simple positives. When I drive to work, there are
horses that only sometimes peek over the fence. When they are there, I
tell my students and that is a positive note for my day.

Picture an inviting atmosphere of quiet, calming music playing to set
the mood as the students enter the classroom each morning. A daily routine to begin and guide the children is natural and inviting. Students
each have a "positive thoughts book" that they write in first thing each

day. They usually have so much to say but all they are asked to do is to write something positive. These entries jump-start the day's journey on a positive note. They feel comfortable to be in "their" classroom and channel their thoughts to something positive. Everyone can find something positive, even on a gloomy day (as in, maybe we will see a rainbow?). A positive beginning sets the tone for an entire day for the child, fellow classmates, and . . . yes—the teacher! This quick daily experience needs only a brief teacher comment or happy face. I respond daily with a short written response that continues the momentum as they write back to me. I return the positive thoughts book at the end of each day because tomorrow is always a new day.

This progressive experience can begin with only pictures, developing with dictation for the very young. The growth shows as children develop their writing and thinking skills along with confidence and maturity. As you "reach" and "stretch" the students, help them to discover (and use) a good attitude. Once, a newly enrolled child ran in late and burst out loudly, "I have nothing positive to say!" All looked up curiously, yet with understanding, and said, "You got here and that's positive!"

Now grown, Stan remembers, "Many things were going on in my young life. It was difficult to begin those days. Sometimes my motivation to go to school was to hear the music and to know I was appreciated for me! That was my 'positive' and a better day would begin."

This energy flows within the classroom and weaves into your every lesson. I believe we can always find something positive in everything we do and I instill this in my students. When you do this, watch success soar as students feel good about who they are.

Once children grasp confidence, then they feel they can take on the world. Suddenly, problems are not so big and tasks no longer seem unattainable. Self-esteem helps students grow and develop at their own levels while feeling good about each and every accomplishment. Sometimes you might see students just reading through their own positive thoughts book remembering special moments and focusing on happiness.

How special when June approaches, for children and families (and teacher, too) to review the progress made day by day! This is a positive memory of a school year, and a gift for all. It can also be a positive beginning and transition if you incorporate the same system in your class (and school) the next year. How smooth when the first day of the next school year begins familiar and positive for all!

Former student Mr. Ken Hokana, now grown with a college degree and his own business, says: "I have wonderful memories of our many fun learning experiences. I liked the many decorations that we made and displayed with pride to make up our room environment. Your class was like fantasyland, always enticing us to learn fabulous things. What I *especially* loved was the daily writing we did because you invited us to pick any topic we wanted to write about!"

HOW TO DO THIS?

You can use a teacher-made log or a composition book. Students may write about *any* topic of their choice. This conveys teacher approval of who they are. A healthy sense of self begins and written responses develop with a positive outlook. The writing needs to be positive. To encourage the process and momentum, you (the teacher) are obliged to write back! It can be just a special happy face or a short one-word (one sentence) response. Students read them and build the connection with you because you are becoming part of (understanding) their "world." No corrections from the teacher—this is their time to write/flow/express their inner thoughts.

Writing in a positive thoughts book is a routine to begin your every day. Students know the expectation is to walk into class and write something *positive*. Even five-year-olds begin to discuss something special to illustrate on the way to school. It is okay to let the students pick their topic! They are developing and thinking, and you are establishing a relationship as well as their future. Students are being trained to look at the bright side of life!

Students and teacher begin to focus on strengths rather than weaknesses. This is encouraging and inspirational for both. This is a model to induce self-esteem.

Debora Phillips' *How to Give Your Child a Great Self-Image* provides a message to parents that applies to all of us: "You have a lot of things to teach your child in the next few years: how to talk, how to crawl, how to use a fork and spoon, how to read, how to tie a shoelace, how to play baseball. . . . Is how to have a great self-image on your list? While all the other things can wait, teaching your child how to have a great self-image can't" (Phillips 1989).

OTHER STEPS TO SELF-ESTEEM

Ongoing Class Discussions: Help your students grasp an understanding that all students are equal. Students of any age are sensitive and the feeling of absolute "belonging" is what they need. There is no favoritism; there is compassion and empathy for each other. An environment encouraging self-esteem is a classroom in which students thrive. When the students understand that everyone is an individual with strengths and weaknesses, they are ready to begin learning. We all have students who are in and out of the classroom for specialists and special needs. Establish a climate that this is something to appreciate and you are fostering the acceptance and approval of each other.

Lunch Bunch: My goal is for each and every student to be responsible, independent, and happy! Years ago, students asked me, "If you are trying to create a 'family' atmosphere for understanding and learning, then why don't you ever eat with us?" Because of this, what started immediately was a positive "building" technique for strengthening student-teacher relationships that automatically spills into student work. Lunch becomes a positive reinforcement when students are invited to eat with their teacher! Weekly, once a month, or whatever works, this is an easy "happening" that is reassuring, special, and rewarding. In anticipation, students designed "luncheon invitations" for the teacher to invite those students exhibiting a consistent positive attitude (or whatever guideline you choose to devise: work habits, perhaps, or assignments in).

Activities Promoting Self-Esteem: Beginning of the year assignments that stress students' attributes accentuate the positives. Suggested Assignments: A self-portrait (possibly to include words written/listed indicative of personal traits/likes/interests), a "mirror" poster of positive traits students see about themselves, a mobile with "pieces" reflecting pieces of a students life, a pennant with the student name in bold letters and characteristics surrounding in either words or pictures, a collage with cut-out pictures from magazines about personal qualities/likes (also can include personal photographs), or an advertisement "spelling out" the qualities of a student. Whatever activities you and your students select, be sure to complete the assignment about you as well—not as a sample, but as a way of completing an assignment "with" them so that they begin to know about who you are too!

IT'S HOW YOU SAY IT!

I attended a conference in a classroom that was ready and awaiting the excitement of a new school year. As I sat there, I found my mind wandering. The presenter shared expertise, "When you teach, it is a good idea to jot down who has trouble. . . . If a child finishes early, let them pull out a book and read. Nothing else! They are to disturb no one." I could only think about how a child would feel! What about taking note of those who have mastery and need enrichment? How about a quiet learning activity to stimulate the accelerating child without rigidity? Clearly posted were the standards: "Anything below 70 percent will require a parent signature. Anything below 59 percent, you fail. No excuses!" No amount of room decorations could erase this negativity. Why not a "Do your best!" Or, "Anything above 70 percent, we will applaud!"

As an educator, the message you most want to convey is praise and the appreciation and acceptance of individuality. Facilitate an understanding that we are alike and different! Inspire your students to develop their own talents. The interpretation of individuals should be celebrated, not analyzed. I find every class to have its own personality. It is up to you, the teacher, to build the relationships while inviting student cooperation and acceptance. Educators today are faced with raising the standards and scores. If you create a community so the dynamics for students are more positive and comfortable, there is a natural pendulum movement to meet and go beyond the expectations. As you build self-esteem, you lay the foundation that encourages higher student interest, ongoing development, and genuine satisfaction.

MY VERY FAVORITE SELF-ESTEEM BUILDING ACTIVITIES

A star in Hollywood! Have each student make a star as if they are Hollywood's favorite new discovery. Use a large piece of paper or poster because handprints and footprints are a must. This is a special way to create a positive room environment that is colorful, individual, and honoring every student!

Help each student to make a set of fingerprints and display them in the classroom alongside their name. This is a visual way to observe the similarities, differences, and uniqueness of student names and fingerprints. For fun, you can also use fingerprints to make people and animal pictures and characters. With the fingerprints as the base, all kinds of concoctions can be created. This evolves into fun and creative stories to write, share, and display!

Make a pattern for an "academy award" (or students can design their own). This project allows students to reveal wonderful things about themselves and why they should win an academy award.

Students can draw (or bring) a suitcase. Fill it with messages or clues to communicate effectively "who" they are.

Ask students to make a résumé. Explain that they should "put their best foot forward" by focusing the attention on their outstanding qualities.

When you teach self-esteem, you open many doors for your students. A struggling young man told me, "Tell someone they are not the only ones who don't have it. Self-esteem is when you do something you can't do and you never give up. I didn't have it . . . until . . . I did!"

Being positive is a nurturing teaching style that contributes to student success. Inevitably, each student brings with them their "baggage" and external influences, bad or good. Encouraging student development includes giving appropriate praise for student participation and work. To acknowledge even the smallest accomplishment gives positive recognition and a desire to forge ahead. Students grow and learn together in a continuous process. As knowledge is cultivated and acquired, self-esteem and confidence strengthen.

SOME CHILDREN'S THOUGHTS

"A lot of people don't have self-esteem. If people get screamed at or don't get compliments, they don't feel good about themselves. When you have self-esteem you can do your schoolwork better because you feel confident." (Jesse, age 7)

"Believe in yourself. I believe in myself because I try and try again until I get it. This gives me a lot of pride. Pride is when you are proud of yourself or someone else. Positive means something good. I like when good stuff happens." (Brigette, age 8)

"Self-esteem is something that makes you glad inside. You can't have self-esteem unless you have self-respect. Some feelings people get when they have self-esteem are happy, glad, positive, bloom with joy, and feeling good about yourself. I have self-esteem. You can have self-esteem if you believe in yourself." (Charlene, age 7)

"There are some people who do not have self-esteem, but you can give it to them. You can help them and tell them they can do it. If you do not have self-esteem, I want to tell you to try to have it. You can find it!" (Miriam, age 9)

"Self-esteem is feeling good about yourself. I can give self-esteem to other people by telling them about it and making them happier about themselves." (Jade, age 9)

Patricia Ison surprised me years later by reappearing one day in my classroom with her college degree and said: "Little people with big dreams need to be encouraged to realize their potential. When you are young (and older), you need to believe in yourself, but first people need to make you aware that they believe in you. Then you grow without the need for constant reassurance."

Tricia Roach (now Patricia Ison) in fifth grade.

UPPER-GRADE ASSISTANTS
CAN GIVE TO YOUNGER STUDENTS

Robin Benson, an older student, said:

It was amazing to walk into a classroom where I could be me. I could have bad days, my brother could have bad days, and still there was a smiling face to greet me. I didn't have to explain why I got in trouble for talking, I just had to say I was sorry and move on. We would talk about the positive things going on, like Grandma and Grandpa coming to visit, and why I looked forward to that. We talked about Mom coming home early that one day . . . not about all the times she had to work late. We focused on the good things, when most everyone else wanted to talk through the bad. I remember being loved and wanted as I would work in Ms. Gail's class. I loved working with the kids and seeing them light up when I told them I was proud if they got through a page in a book. That is how she taught me to help the kids. . . . Even if it took the entire recess to get them through a sentence, I told them how good they did. It seemed weird at the time, I remember thinking it took them so long to read a dumb sentence, what is good about that? Now I know and I know that is how I was changed. Someone took me in and instead of wanting to know why something wasn't an A, I was praised about the work that I had done. So many times now I think about that, and how my life is different.

I try to look at people with a positive attitude, because someone did that for me. My dream is to change kids' lives, to believe in them. I have started my teaching degree at the University of Oregon. When I have a child, I pray that the people it will come in contact with during his or her life will have that same guidance and the same positive attitude I was able to experience. I hope that my child will want to make a difference in someone's life, because someone made a difference in theirs.

SOMETIMES CHILDREN GIVE EACH OTHER SELF-ESTEEM

Cross-aged tutoring in a comfortable setting can increase self-esteem for everyone involved. I think healthy self-esteem takes place for children when there is a balance. We took young children facing many challenges in life and blended them with older students in search of self-esteem. Together, they shared attitudes, behaviors, and successful accomplishments. They accepted each other's strengths and weaknesses while enjoying working together. While children interacted and shared their experiences, there was also a boost towards healthy self-esteem.

Ms. Rhoda Vestuto, a speech pathologist, explains:

> I needed supervision for one small group of children while I did intensive remediation with others in my preschool communication handicapped class. We did not choose the 'stars' of Gail's class, but rather older children who, for various reasons, were in need of attention and support. The older children understood that their responsibility was truly needed. They had the admiration, respect, and fondness of the little ones. Their achievements gave them a sense of fulfillment. They experienced the joy that comes from giving to others and knowing its value. The younger children were given appropriate models to emulate who was somewhat close to their own age. They were able to identify with the positive feelings that the older children were emanating. They were liked and accepted for themselves. They experienced entrée into the world of older children usually perceived as the "power," who became, in essence, their peers. They had, in a school setting, relief from interaction with the teaching adult and competitive peers.
>
> I've had the opportunity to speak to some of the older and younger children several years after they participated in this program and I can testify to the impression it made on them. The greatest assets were the intangibles and lifelong, unique memories that now belong to each of them. (Vesuto 2001)

IT SEEMED TO ME LIKE THE NATURAL THING TO DO

To me, the relationship between a teacher and a student models an enthusiasm for learning. A child identifies with the teacher's attitude seeking conscientious work and including self-motivation. When a teacher is stimulating, this builds on a student's internal motivation to do his or her best to acquire competence. Rather than being negative, the best strategy is to provide alternate solutions and supportive ways to focus and improve.

Former student Mrs. Ison shared the expression "red ink":

As a student, it is really discouraging to get your paper back with red ink all over it. It makes the student focus on the negative, instead of the positive parts of their work. In fourth grade, Gail referred to our first effort as a rough draft and wrote suggestions in the margin that were helpful in editing our work to make it even better than we had originally thought. Then we were ready to find the errors and complete our projects with pride and a sense of accomplishment instead of disappointment. I think for me it actually got the creative juices flowing.

Dr. Phillips poses a question:

What do you want your child to be? There may be days when you want her to be tall, rich, an astronaut, a star, a gourmet chef, a doctor, lawyer, a millionaire. But what you really want your child to be is happy. The happiest people you know don't necessarily have the best jobs, or the most money, or even the best health. Their "secret," as you may already know, is self-esteem. They feel lovable, valuable, worthy. They have the strength to deal with life's inevitable setbacks. They're happy because they're happy with themselves. That's why you want your child to have a great self-image." (Phillips 1989, 4)

Quality/positive attention assures student acceptance, respect, and recognition as an accepted human being. When you instill the desire in children, they will begin to be the best they can be. Isn't this all we can ask for? Every educator's hope? This can bring about extraordinary students pursuing their education (and future) with fervent responsibility and zest.

Random selections of young children's positive thoughts:

Tommrow, I can't wait till first day of science.

Today I have Chess. Tommorrow is the cultural arts Festabble.

I'm fine. so is mom and dad. I'm getting the hang of it. This is a real cool class. I cant wate intil tommro so I can relly orstand the clas.

I hope I make a lot of friends this year.

Where potting up are new fence. I like to wach them. If isgoing to be wood. I said "hi" to the work men. We are remodling our house.

I woke up at 6:01. I was exited (uase I got to see my freandes!

Yesterday I called Stephiny and I talked to her. that was cool. I am having a really good week.

Dear Ms Gail, I am glad you are back Ms Gail. I really missed you.

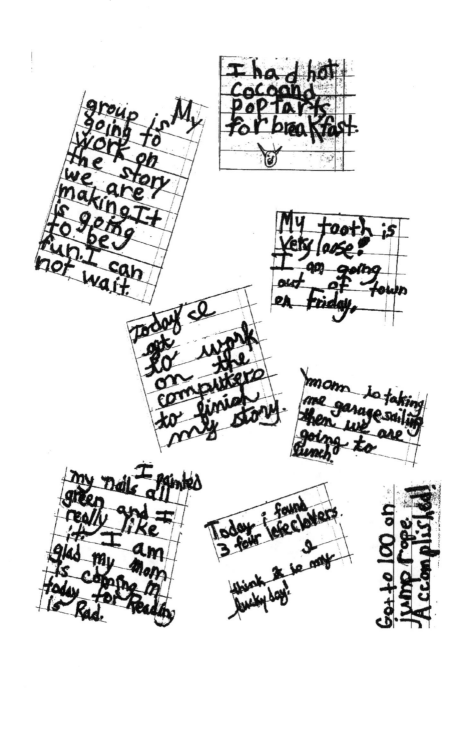

I had hot cocoa and poptarts for breakfast.

group is My going to work on the story we are making. It is going to be fun. I can not wait.

My tooth is very loose! I am going out of town on Friday.

Today I get to work on the computers to finish my story.

mom is taking me garage sailing then we are going to lunch.

I painted my nails all green and I really like it. I am glad my mom is coming in today for Reading is Rad.

Today I found 3 four leafclovers. I think it is my lucky day!

Got to 100 on jump rope. Accomplished!

On the week-
end my
sister had
a tea party on
the ash and
i wore a beautiful
deross with
lase. We had
ordervs and
cookys. We
playd scrabl.
i was the
oldest.

Dear
Positive
Thoghts.
Today I
sharpened
the pencils.
I brang
a big jar
Of peanuts
for Ms. Gail
Our theme
is "Be Yourself"
The weekend
was very
nice.
We praticed
our inchworm
play. I did
not know
what todo
...like a clueless
little inchworm!

Today my dad
stay home
with my
brother.

Dear Ms. Gail,
Yesterday I got
new colothes
and they were
old and I really
like them. I
had a lot
of fun on
the swings.

I'm good at
jummp ropeing.

I really love
this class.

Today is
Halloween
night.

I am happy because I am back from beaing sick, and I am happy Today! I am going to Play With my friends Today.

Yesterday I went to a dodgers game and we stayaed up till 10 o'clock and we were in the first row.

Today, my mom is coming to help.

I was the first person to get up in my family!

I'm sure that I'm going to have fun.

I'm happy that tomorrow is testing, its going to be very fun tomorrow.

Today it's raining!

Today in our classroom we have a substitute. She is nice.

Dear Positive thoughts, Today is my Birthday, I'm turning nine!!!!

Tomorrow I get to go to Santa Maria to baby-sit little kids.

I feel positive some of my quarters have a Philedelphia sign instead of a D.C. Sign.

Dear Ms.Gail, I am glad that I got my glasses yesterday.

⑤

CHOICES

Teaching is a commitment. It is un-conditional. One does not teach for the money or the vacation days. I think deep down it is with the hope of reaching out to children and inspiring nonstop learn-ing. If you truly love what you are doing, then and only then will it reflect on your students. You begin with hopes and dreams and it is the relationships you build with your students that make  the difference. The link between a teacher and a student will help them to make choices when needed to redirect or rediscover, to be more productive in their endeavors.*

Every day is a challenge and no two days are ever the same. No two children are the same. A teacher making the choice to also be a student is a valuable quality because we learn so much from our students. I am who I am today because of them. These kids are my life! They enrich me!

Be supportive as you blend many elements into your teaching style. Academic mastery will escalate along with laughter and students performing at their personal best. Help them open doors, walk down avenues, and cross bridges. Our attitudes and passions influence students to take "baby steps" and reach their milestones. Nurture and reassure your students as you help them to find their passion.

A teacher is like a coach. Help every child get "off that bench," to believe in himself or herself, and you might just discover a star! A teacher's best reward is seeing how you affect each child!

PATIENCE

Pictures of mountains—hills, mounds, big ones, small ones, elevations of every size. Dark, obscure, concealed, and why would a young child only draw mountains? As an educator, it is important to remember that different things have different meanings to each of us. Though I was puzzled, I made the choice to observe with interest and to compliment him for completing a minimal task. He was making a choice to draw something!

His first day of "real" school, he stood frozen by my door. We tried to understand him. It was neither English nor Spanish and seemed like a conglomeration of languages. And it was. Little William finally did make the choice to enter the classroom. From afar, he watched everything we did, and he listened. William was not pushed or pulled but allowed to enter according to his own comfort and confidence level. This gave him the opportunity to learn trust slowly and to realize that it was up to him to make his own choices. He had the freedom to discover himself with confidence. It was day by day that young William (age six) seemed to build a foundation step by step.

All individuals have something to say. The other thirty-two students listened when he tried to express himself. They made the choices to include and help him, which further led to his confidence that generated satisfaction. A smile is communication and so is humor, complete with shared laughter. They put manipulatives one way, and he moved them another.

He was, however, productive, contributing, and experiencing new things. Everything was new and different for William. We included him as students learned phonetic sounds and words. We used pictures for William to comprehend the stories and studies. As he watched, he made more and more choices to participate. The choices William was able to make about his own learning gave him a sense of personal power that perhaps he never had. This was a totally new environment to him and as he gradually learned to trust those around him, including his teacher, he took greater risks toward becoming a part of the group. I monitored his progress and observed measurable academic growth. When students understand it is "okay to be different," they can also appreciate each other's success.

Physical education at an early level is really a subject of mere participation. (And, oh, he did!) While he didn't understand the rules, William loved to enter in on the fun, yet would somehow take the ball and run the other way! Gradually, accomplishments showed in all areas and the gleam in his eyes exuded mastery of even the simplest concept. Positive choices and a collaborative environment will bring out the best in every student.

Before long, comprehension became apparent, along with the mastery of many skills. English grew from words to sentences and the choice for nonstop communication enlightened us all. We began to understand that his "language" was a mixture. William's family came from the Czech Republic. Their passports were confiscated. They fled to Yugoslavia with William on their back. His family took risks and made the choice to never give up. After close to a year of living in the Austrian Alps, the family was granted asylum and able to enter the United States of America.

So William really did know all about mountains! Indeed, when William verbalized that he lived in the mountains, he truly did. So many choices this family had endured.

Little William eventually grew into the amazing person he is today and now weighs 270 lbs, and is six feet seven. He made many choices and is now at Stanford University on a scholarship. Today "Will" is an All-American, a member of Sports Hall of Fame, and was named to the California All-Star Football Classic for which he played in the Rose Bowl. He is a multitalented athlete excelling with national attention and champion titles in not only football but also basketball, track, and shot put and was a two-time national decathlon champion. Those choices to discover new things, day by day and step by step, brought Will to be a member of the California Scholastic Federation.

William recalls:

I have always been a curious child. From the beginning, I learned that there was no such thing as a stupid question. My parents always asked many questions and they encouraged me to do the same. I think that asking questions is critical to a child's growth. Every child learns and develops in a different way, so therefore they need to ask questions to help them adapt in the learning situation. For myself, asking questions for you to explain something in the way I could understand was my way of learning.

I will never forget the day I was able to read that book completely. I remember one day in class I just opened up the book and started reading it. It seemed like all the pieces of the puzzle came together and everything clicked. I then brought the book to you to show you that I could read it and you were so proud of my progress. I ran home enthusiastically to show my parents my reading capability. I still cannot explain how all of a sudden my reading came together. But it was like a light bulb came on. I think teachers just need to be patient with their

Young William Svitek.

William Svitek: high school honor student.

William Svitek at Stanford.

students. I was trying very hard all along. It just took me longer than some students. If some people understood my background, coming from a non-English-speaking household, then they could understand how it took longer for me. I always remained positive and took a hard-working approach to my learning.

I never considered myself as disadvantaged. I always thought that I was just as smart and talented as everybody else. I had positive self-esteem! I feel so fortunate to have teachers like you who care about their student's growth. You are one of the reasons why I am now at Stanford University. Thank you for everything you have done for me and believing in me.

YOUNG CLARA

She thought no one cared, that no one would notice if she went away. Now she shares why one day she made a choice:

Clara portrays Annie Oakley.

> I used to listen to everyone. They shared their day, their thoughts, and their hopes! I had my own too. This made me think. Before I couldn't talk because I thought I wasn't so special. It took two or three years for my friends to encourage me. Then one day I thought that if they can all talk and share, why don't I? I finally felt accepted that I could speak to others just like everyone else! I just . . . did it! I knew they were listening to what I had to say and I felt a sudden overwhelming sensation.

A "TEACHER REWARD"

Many years later, a folded piece of paper was placed into my hands at a holiday party. I wish I had read it at that moment instead of when I got home because it was truly a gift to treasure. Former student Eric See wrote:

> There is never a day that goes by that I don't have to make a choice. Every time I make one of those decisions, whether it be what to wear, what to eat, or what to do, I am guided by something I was taught when I was in first grade—that I am unique and special.
>
> When I am faced with one of these decisions, I know that whatever I choose I will feel proud, because I am me. I know that whichever choice I choose is the best one because the best choice is the one that best suits me. I know that I need not conform to other's standards and views.
>
> In first grade, our class performed Readers Theatre plays. I was the Papa Bear. I quickly adopted my own way of playing the Papa Bear. I

spoke in my own best deep gruff voice and did my very best to portray Papa Bear. We performed the plays at a local college. I could have easily strayed from my melodramatic portrayal of Papa Bear for fear that others would laugh at me. I did not! I made a choice. I remembered that lesson that I was unique and special and the best way was my way. It is something I will carry through with me my entire life

Eric See studying script to be Papa Bear.

Eric See grown.

Teachers direct and influence students with the myriad of topics taught each and every day. When students can complete an educational assignment without outside direction, you know they have successfully grasped the material that you have led them to acquire. Be *in* the moment! Don't underestimate how your caring, smile, or compliment can touch a student's life. When you have a connection with each other, students will open up more and reach for the best they can do. If your students recognize that you believe what you are teaching is important, they will naturally improve and put in the extra effort.

Take cues from kids so you know if they understand and how well they learn. Be responsive to your students; be attuned if what you are giving them is developmentally appropriate. We spend so much time "teaching." It is also essential to know how to give them suggestions; to steer them to reason and figure out things for themselves. By "doing," children delve into projects and contribute to their learning, and also reap the reward of skill achievement. Choices help you grow. Invite success into your student's lives so they can make choices and seek aspirations.

Use those special "teachable moments!" If you include students in evaluating their work and progress, you are helping them to make choices of how to improve to reach satisfaction and success. Yes, "testing" is done throughout the "system," but we need to remember that our objective is the learning that takes place.

Young children enter their first day of school with genuine excitement and anticipation. My goal is to encourage this energy and keep this spirit alive in all of my students. As a teacher you affect your students, and I think this influence never stops.

World-renowned William Glasser believes that "Choice Theory is based on the belief that the only person whose behavior each of us can control is ourself. Education is not acquiring knowledge; it is best defined as using knowledge. An important purpose of education is to nurture a love for lifelong learning in all students" (Glasser 1999). No one can make the students think—but we can encourage children to clearly express themselves and make the decision to do the best that they can do!

In his book *Choice Theory*, Glasser states, "We do not answer a phone because it rings; we answer it because we want to. Every time we answer a phone, we have decided that this is the best choice. If we didn't think so, we wouldn't answer it." Thus, the behavior we choose is generated inside our brains.

My favorite of Dr. Glasser's thoughts is: "Fun is the genetic reward for learning. With the possible exception of whales and porpoises, we are the only creatures who play all our lives. And because we do, we learn all our lives. The day we stop playing is the day we stop learning."

IN THE BOX

The delivery of a large, unwanted empty box literally opens doors. It is you who creates the doors and windows and the community of your students who paint the box to fascinate all. When children have the opportunity to write a story or silently read a book, a choice where they do it can make the difference. A quiet corner, a seat on the floor, or a retreat into a cardboard box. It's amazing what a nonproducing child can accomplish while sitting in a decorated box "in their own world." I've never understood this, but if you place a few such boxes in your classroom, you will understand what I mean.

Making choices follows the concept that education should involve useful learning. Choices are the important skills that students take with them to use for a lifetime. Along with this, Glasser maintains that "All we can give or get from other people is information. How we deal with that information is our or their choice. A teacher can give a student information and help him or her to use the information, but the teacher can't do the work for the student."

CHOICES MY STUDENTS MAKE ON A DAILY BASIS

- I ask parents to encourage children to select their own clothes (no matter how interesting or unusual the outfits might be!)
- Where to sit
- Who to sit by in circle
- What to write in positive thoughts book
- What book to read for silent reading
- Not to stop or give up
- How to budget time and when to do homework ~ for it is due weekly (not daily)
- Who to sit near during classwork
- What (if anything) to contribute in circle
- What to include in the daily communicator
- Where to sit to read it
- Make good use of free time

STUDENTS ARE ENCOURAGED TO SEEK CHOICES THAT WILL PRODUCE COMPETENCE IN ACADEMICS

Kendra at second grade clearly defined "choices" in a way that really explains it all:

Choices are different. Some are important and some hardly make a change in the world. Choices can range from when Napoleon had to decide whether to keep or set free over one thousand Turkish prisoners of war to whether you want to name a character in a story Tom, Tim, Bob, or

Kendra Yoshinaga

Ben. Some choices can be hard to make, such as if your best friend has a birthday party, but if that party starts and ends right at the same time as when you have a family picnic, what would you do? Some people would say "Go to the picnic." Others would say, "Go to the party." I would say it would be best to leave the party early and then go to the picnic. Life is full of choices. There are big choices and little choices, important choices, and choices that hardly make a difference."

TEACHER CHOICE ... TO PARTICIPATE

"It's all your fault! You go to carnivals, meetings, and do 'things' beyond the hours of the school day. We are so underpaid. How can we get better benefits or raises if people like you appear satisfied by working extra hours? You put too much into your teaching!" Unexpectedly one day, a teacher yelled this at me! At first I felt so attacked, yet as the day went on the scenario took on meaning.

Are you there for your students? You can't just shut it off when the clock says 3 p.m. To get the results, become a part of your student's lives. If your school has an after-school function and your students have a booth or a song to sing, it seems logical you would choose to participate, which makes a positive statement. The students relate to you and it is more exciting for them when they see you care and are supportive. When you put more into it, you get more out of it—especially when you see their faces shine when they see you show up.

Some teachers get caught up in a routine—just go to work and go home. It is my hope that educators will take time to rededicate themselves as to why they became teachers in the first place. If you begin to shut down, how do you expect your students to open up? When educators make the choice to make changes in their students, they are also changing as a teacher. When you are creative within yourself, it comes back to you immeasurably. Don't lose the focus of why you became a teacher: to be there for your students. Look inside yourself to the enchantment.

I can tell you that teaching to me is more than just a job. It is taking a dramatic role in children's lives, for now and the future. I have worried, laughed, and cried with students. Teachers who explore opportunity invite students to do the same. Give them hope, have them tell you their dreams, and to face challenges.

You won't have discipline problems or negativity in the classroom if you go that extra mile of giving to your kids. They will learn more and you will be fulfilled. Aren't those the reasons you got into teaching in the first place? The true fringe benefit of teaching is the reward of students becoming independent thinkers who take the steps to grow and to flourish. I don't think the matter of minutes I put in matters as much as the experiences. I am doing, they are doing, and intangible benefits unfold when you see and share the positive changes in your students.

An example of an individual who gained learning experiences as he reached to the positives to become a complete person is John Hill, Los Angeles County chief of staff for Supervisor Yvonne Brathwaite Burke. He speaks openly about turning negative into positive. He tells of day-dreaming and searching for an outlet. Books became the only consistency in his life so he chose to devour everything in print, from books to newspapers to magazines.

> Don't become your environment, only learn from it. I attended about ten different schools and I had a difficult time adjusting to these environments and new kids. I was extremely shy. I would fight anyone who said a word to me. When I needed to shut out my surroundings, I would go somewhere by myself and read. Books were my sustenance, they gave me hope of a better life, a life beyond the cotton fields, vineyards, and peach orchards. (Hill, 11)

He made choices!
"Ultimately" states Dr. Glasser in *Every Student Can Succeed,*

> Everything I suggest in this book is based on how you and your students feel and that given a choice, both you and they would rather feel good than bad. Or would rather be happy than sad. This means that when you have difficulty teaching a student, one thing you can be absolutely sure of is that student is unhappy in your class and, very likely, unhappy in school. And if you are unsuccessful in dealing with him, the same could be said of you. (Glasser 2000, 4–5)

Glasser states that his suggestions are risk-free. He is looking for joy—the joy of learning! "If you can relate to them differently, they may start to behave differently and this difference may make your job both easier and more successful. In other words, by dealing with them differently, they may become more interested in doing more for you than they're doing now" (Glasser 1999, 41).

He believes that when students like you and when they see a sense in what you are trying to teach, then they will perform. This "connection" brings the joy of learning, happiness, and success.

When children are internally motivated, they will make choices. Their behaviors are chosen in an attempt to achieve their wants. In a need-fulfilling environment, modeling and consistency lead to positive change and learning. In a quality environment, there is trust, communication, and ongoing changes. Invite your students to see things for themselves. A noncoercive relationship between a student and teacher leads to the implementation of useful and real learning. If students give 100 percent of their effort, they are doing their best and fulfilling their needs. This is satisfying and the core of building successful lives. It is up to the teacher to provide an enhanced environment while helping students discover that education will enrich their future.

WHY STUDENTS WROTE THE "RULES"

"Boy . . . girl . . . boy . . . girl . . . Stand here. . . . Sit there. . . . Sit. . . . Quiet. . . . Now!" were the resounding words I heard teachers shouting to nearby students when my class was amidst others on a field trip.

My students eyes saw it, their ears heard it, and that memory stuck. (I don't know what you call it—impatience, burn out, control?) Why does a teacher behave in such a fashion? What happened to being a role model? The louder you scream, the less they will hear and the more they will shut down. You can reach others more by talking with them, maintaining respect, and establishing a relationship. As an adult, how can you make it better for children? Give them a chance. They can do it!

This unfortunate occurrence not only impacted my students but opened my eyes, too. It stayed with them the next day in discussions. They questioned why other students had to even experience such a thing! They wondered if it happened every day? Thought-provoking student writings developed into "rules" for teachers; a meaningful guideline for of us:

"Don't scream . . . you don't want us to."
"Don't yell at us . . . we will react . . . talk to us."
"Don't show your anger . . . it escalates ours."
"I don't want to be afraid . . . don't make me be."
"Work with me . . . I will work with you."
"Connect . . . we are here together."
"Listen . . . do you really hear what we are saying?"
"Look at us . . . how do we feel? . . . what do we think?"
"If you truly listen . . . I will talk."
"Give support . . . and I will participate."
"If you are excited . . . so will I be."
"If you start an interest . . . I will find it.
"If I know you will comment (or react) . . . I will give."
"Learn from us . . . as we learn from you."
"If I am happy . . . I will learn more."

CREATE THE CHOICE TO LEARN IN YOUR CLASSROOM

Help students to use the knowledge that you give them. If you present it to them so they know it has meaning and is useful in their lives, they will make the choice to be more attentive. Demonstrate! Give them the opportunity to interpret, to practice, to contribute to the process, to participate! A good foundation is when children acquire the knowledge of how to question, analyze, and find answers (and the desire to want to find the answers). Encourage them. Engage them with clues, student interaction, and listening skills. Isn't it true if something is interesting, you want to know more? Memorization is not teaching. Sometimes the best positive learning comes from clarification, repetition, and variety. The application makes changes because new ideas become processed and become a part of us. Encourage students not to compete with each other but to do their very best. True learning becomes alive and is such a gratifying experience. If children learn, if they truly digest what you are teaching them, they become confident—which leads to competence. If you get to the point where you want to know the "special" qualities in your students, you will have the key to being a great teacher. They will unlock that special place, with your help—a skill they discover in themselves.

I PERSONALLY WOULD LIKE TO SAY

There are choices every student should be able to make: Read for the pleasure of reading, learn to find out what is not known, seek the joy of discovering, accept challenge, evolve, have freedom in self-expression (oral and written), continue to redefine and expand, utilize talents and interests . . . and seek them, be able to relax and concentrate, observe and make changes if or when necessary.

Create . . . explore . . . examine . . . experiment . . . design . . . improvise . . . adapt . . . notice . . . stretch . . . experience . . . !

"CHOICE" BY SKY MCLEOD, AGE EIGHT

You can make a choice every second of all days, in a million different ways
From when you write a paper, what the next letter will be
To when you look around, where you want to see
A judgment or preference is what it means.
If you couldn't make a choice, you could not walk, talk, see, or be!
Some are big, some are quite small
Only you can't see them at all!

THEIR CHOICES?

Give them the tools, help them to recognize and want to attain these:

A positive attitude	A vision
Patience	Opportunity
Desire	Responsibility
Connect	Appreciation
Understanding	Improve

Focus	Grow
Ask questions	Respect
Seek answers	Independence
Persistence	Mastery
Do your best	Learning is nonstop
Awareness	Purpose
Curiosity	Self-fullfillment
Self-examination	Pride
Determination	Interest
Attitude	Laughter
One day at a time	Pleasure

Always be "You"

6

CIRCLE

*When students are calm, have gotten
"out" of their system that which
might inhibit learning, education climbs to new heights.
Students can better focus on
what a teacher is saying because they have gotten
beyond their worries so
they are better able to
strive for performance and
reaching their full potential.*

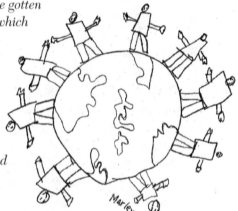

We looked into each other's eyes.
(We didn't speak a word of the same language.) I smiled. I tried hand
motions. I wrote on the chalkboard *Malibu, Hollywood, California*? My
audience stared blankly at me. On this morning, I felt "alone" in a classroom filled with fifty high school students in Japan, including the
teacher who spoke not a word of English. At that moment, an interpreter poked her head in the door and I motioned for translation, for
help! With a smile she nodded, said, "you're doing great," and was gone.

I've always believed that communication is the secret ingredient and this was a true challenge. Finally, I laughed, they laughed, and it was clearly evident that laughter is the universal language.

They sat in silence in traditional rows. They looked to me, honored guest, to do something, so with hand gestures I asked them to stand up. I began to push and shove desks and they followed. The desks became arranged into a closed circle. The students sat down a little bewildered and for the first time, not in rows but in a silent circle. I remember motioning with my hands trying to explain *I talk, you talk, we all talk, we share*. Dialogue is not a usual experience because they have been taught to listen, study, and prepare for examinations.

The interpreter reappeared and looked to me with curiosity about the unusual circular configuration. I briefly explained to her the success of communication, students expressing their thoughts. Only one person speaks at a time in a circle, peers listen, with no judgment. Rules were explained in Japanese but the students just looked at each other in silence. The silence of these moments was eventually broken as a significant transformation began. There I was, quiet, listening to a foreign language, the sounds, and inflections of their voices as interaction began.

As a Fulbright Memorial Scholar, I visited schools in Japan. I was intrigued at the students serving and eating "school lunches" together in the classrooms, unsupervised. Some wore masks, aprons, and gloves as they served their fellow students; all ate the same kind of food. They shared the procedure involving me, serving me and sharing their ways. At a certain time, music played over the loudspeaker system and suddenly, all the students stopped eating and stood up. Trashcans were filled and emptied, desks were shoved to a corner, boards and erasers were cleaned, and brooms swiftly swept. They just did it! This is part of the daily routine and curriculum, and school custodians are unknown.

On this day, though, things changed! In the circle, students began to talk about a subject, which surfaced that had never been touched on previously. Clean up! Quiet chatter became fast spoken words. I got the gist of what they were discussing. Translated to, "Why do I always clean the boards? When did you empty the trash? Can't someone else sweep the floors? I don't like serving the food." I didn't really need the translation as I could feel what was happening. This circle was filled with communication and a beginning.

I continued to tour the high school, observed classrooms, and interacted with staff. At lunch on this day, I went right back to that classroom! Though the chairs were back in the rows, things had changed! They had rotated and taken on different jobs. Students giggled at me with knowing looks and thank yous. This was an international experience! I have always wondered how our entire world could improve if everyone had the tools to truly communicate.

Mai Yamamoto of Japan.

I believe in circle as a daily experience. The classroom students and teacher bond with each other and become a family, a community, as they talk, listen, and develop mutual understanding. Once the tone is understood, circle becomes a way of life and can be successfully done with students of any age. I know: curriculum is full and "there is so much to do." Yes, truthfully, there have been days when the last thing on my mind was to have a circle. All who participate, though, come to understand that when students are comfortable, feeling accepted, and understood, the teaching moments are better addressed because the students are ready to listen and learn.

Why have circle? It was a long day when Dee, usually a consistent child, seemed moody and struggling. She had also argued at recess and no one wanted anything to do with her. As she left that afternoon, I asked her if she wanted to talk or if she needed some extra help. She began to shake and between gasps slowly told me that when Mom came home yesterday, her parents had a huge argument. She was scared, actually terrified. I knew instantly that if I had known this early in the morning, maybe I could have helped her through it. That was thirty-three years ago and the day I decided that verbal communication could and would make a difference to students, and more importantly, to me, the teacher. If only I had known! I orchestrated a way for children to have a vehicle to express themselves freely without the worry of any judgment by peers or teacher. I began a daily experience, which evolved into a circle and has taken place in my classroom every day since. (And, over the years, I have taught every grade level, including college.)

I used to be amazed and shocked at some of the stories I heard. Circle is not a counseling session, but an accepting, comfortable group to listen, share, and dialogue with. There are at least two students every year who are going through unusual, traumatic experiences. Often I ponder about all those students, everywhere, who don't have this safety to discuss their inner thoughts and concerns. I wonder how they keep it all in, or let it out in the wrong way. How different it might be if they could better focus on just what they came to school to learn.

What is circle? Circle is a group experience, a constructive process, in which students sit in a circle and openly dialogue with each other. Communication skills are learned and utilized in this process that can be used throughout a students lifetime. All participants are equal. Students learn to express feelings, to appreciate as well as talk about concerns. They learn to know more about each other, the different inner make-up of others. Circle is a means of discussion that develops trust, empathy, understanding, and more meaningful relationships including friends, classmates, teachers, family, and those one meets in everyday life. Students who participate in circle are more accepting of others and less judgmental. It is a way for individuals to tackle difficult times as well as develop compassion. Problems that seem big suddenly diminish when students realize that others have similar thoughts and concerns. (No student "goes home mad.") Circle can also be a time for classmates to celebrate their differences, hopes, and accomplishments. Together, students can better validate who they are, and especially that it is okay to be who you are. Circle guides young children to be interested in others and to learn at an early age that no one is perfect.

Circle is a powerful experience in which students concentrate and learn to identify with each other. Circle is not a pencil and paper activity and there is no right or wrong statement. It is the ability to talk, to communicate.

Who can do circle? Circle is appropriate for any age. Circle can begin at the young age of kindergarten. (The earlier, the better!) Circle skills utilized in the classroom often extend to develop better communication within the family as well as interpersonal relationships. Circle is a mesh of various backgrounds, religions, nationality, education of parents, and varied family dynamics.

Can circle have an affect on "bullying?" Lack of acceptance or understanding by peers (or a teacher) encourages any child to "act out."

The earlier that "communication" can be experienced, relationships can go above judging others and build upon more acceptance.

When students and teachers hear and accept the open sharing of classmates, they develop empathy and better understanding of who each person truly is. Students develop the courage to verbalize, to speak up in an appropriate manner. As students learn to work together in collaborative activities as well as in social settings, they become more sensitive to other individuals. Circle enables participants to not be ostracized by their peers, but rather to be accepted and understood for their differences. Classroom (school) diversity becomes an element of discussion and a part of the learning component. As barriers break down, so does bullying and the exclusion of "social outcasts." Circle can stop injustice before it builds up.

When do you do circle? Circle as a daily activity is truly the most valuable. When circle is an everyday event, little things don't build up inside of children. However, any circle is better than none. Don't be hesitant . . . just start! Circle done at approximately the same time each day is the most consistent and becomes a part of the day that students learn to look forward to. I recommend approximately twenty-five minutes.

CIRCLE BECOMES A DYNAMIC EXPERIENCE —EVERY CIRCLE IS UNIQUE

Guidelines:

- Sit near a different person each time
- Sit in a circle (though often it looks like an oval)
- Sit so all can see each other
- No cross-discussion
- One person speaks at a time
- Do not judge what someone says or thinks
- Nothing in your hands (unless an object is passed)
- Confidentially—what is said in the circle, stays in the circle
- No put-downs
- No interruptions
- The teacher (leader) calls on the speaker

- Listen to what someone is really saying
- Anyone who wants a turn gets a turn
- The right to not talk at all
- Maintain eye contact
- Parents (depending on classroom chemistry and dynamics) can be included if in the room. Often, volunteer parents share thoughts, observations, and enlightening comments.
- If a visitor is in the classroom, it is up to the children if they want to include the visitor in the privacy of their circle.

The Teacher/Leader/Facilitator: Decide on the physical location for circle: sitting in chairs or on the floor. Circle can be done anywhere. Demonstrate nonjudgment and acceptance of all participants. Develop a rapport. You are guiding verbal participation in which individuals grasp self-awareness as well as compatibility. You are fostering verbal communication.

Include a thought or reflection of your own. Bring positive energy and encouragement to the circle. Guide all participants into the process to focus and listen. Encourage spontaneous discussion. Discuss with students the reason for guidelines. Ask them how they feel when they know they (and others participants) can express their feelings for others to hear and understand.

Select speakers in a random order. As trust grows, so does the meaning and significance of circle. Friendships deepen between people who trust each other. Share a story. Guide as necessary. Sometimes the addition of a little humor or laughter can lighten a heavy topic as comments and personal thoughts or experiences can become quite deep and involved.

Format:

Appreciations: "I appreciate" is a positive statement giving recognition to a particular person, or about a feeling or an event. An example, "I appreciate that our field trip is tomorrow." "I have an appreciation that in this class no one makes fun of me when I go for special help in English."

Concerns: "I have a concern." A concern is a statement about something that is troubling or worrying a child. An example, "I have a concern that the tooth fairy didn't come to my house." "I have a concern that staff on the playground wouldn't listen to my side of the story."

Comment: "I have a comment." Sometimes after a statement is made, another child feels a need for an immediate response. Cross-comments add personal experiences, such as how others have solved similar problems. An example, "I understand how you feel that your Mom forgot your lunch." " It must be sad that your cat disappeared and that happened to me once."

I try to rotate appreciations and concerns because I feel this has a better tone and a more positive outcome. However, we always end with an appreciation!

Students have even called emergency circles too! I remember one child angry at a classmate for hitting her at the drinking fountain. Once discussed, it turned out that the other child had merely brushed her friend's shoulder, not realized it, and the classmate had been furious.

I tried an agenda, where students signed a list of pressing topics. This seemed ideal, until in circle someone shared that they felt pressure by this procedure knowing others were going to discuss something they had done. This is a good example of a mistake. Because of this, I did away with the agenda and the same topics are still discussed anyway.

With young elementary-age children, the rule of only one can talk at a time (and to listen) is sometimes difficult to comply. (Each has so much to say.) I have found that if the rule becomes that one can only talk when a certain object is in his or her hand (such as a beanbag), then turns are better taken and understood. It is fulfilling as an educator to see the difference of a circle from day one of school, in comparison to the later part of the school year. Obviously, the content of discussions changes from age five to twelve and so on, but all students have things to say. Students growing up with doing circle understand the concept, but as their maturity develops so does their need to feel listened to by peers (and teachers and parents).

Variations: Go consecutively around the circle, each individual having a chance to express himself or herself. (This is often excellent when regarding a specific topic or thought.) It must be understood, though, that there is always the right to pass.

When first beginning the circle experience in a class, a specific topic might make it easier to create discussion and comments. Participants need to feel a comfort zone to speak out loud in a nonjudgmental, noncompetitive forum.

A circle of students asking what they want to learn in September, their hopes and goals, is a valuable beginning variation. Suddenly surrounded by others who listen and care, students will become more responsible and aware of how their actions affect one another. Developing trust through positive and significant interpersonal experiences sets the tone for a cooperative group of students. Each child (and the class as a whole) will grow as he or she learns to enjoy communication.

Conducting a circle around a tree or outside at a quiet, natural setting is sometimes stimulating and different.

My favorite "variation" is always the last day of school when students share what they liked best during the school year (their favorite moments, qualities of friendship, how peers have improved). The last circle before summer is very emotional. All participants know that when that circle ends, they will never be the "same family" again. Even returning students, or those in multi-aged classes, recognize that someone moves, someone is new, or a summer experience (good or bad) changes a child. I like to include the parents in the last circle. They can listen and appreciate what their child has experienced in school and amongst fellow students. Often statements evolve from students and parents (or included staff members) about individual growth, accomplishments, memories, and experiences. (Let's face it, the teacher can't remember *everything*, and the concluding circle solidifies so much for a dedicated teacher.)

When a new student who has never been in circle joins a class, it can seem intimidating and unusual to him or her. A peer explains what a circle is and new students are asked merely to listen to what their new friends have to say. Fellow students often welcome them or say something positive about having a new member in the class. Because of the camaraderie, a new student emerges into the class dynamics as if they have always been there and when they are ready, they open up and speak in a circle.

Circle becomes an electric magic that flows amongst the students. I try to cultivate in each and every child the ability to openly reach out and better understand others. Circle is part of any language curriculum and I find that written language also expands as students learn to better express themselves. It is also a living component of social studies. Personal effectiveness promotes academic success. Students become more responsible for their own actions. Interpersonal relations incorporate respect, increase sensitivity, and strengthen a child's self-image. When people like themselves, they are better at relating to others. Circle helps all to incorporate a willingness to listen and a better recognition of how others and circumstances can influence their behaviors, attitude, and outlook on life. Positive energy and enthusiasm lead the way for continuous growth in and out of the classroom.

Circle has helped me, the teacher, in numerous ways. It helps me to better understand the individuality of each and every pupil. Outside of the circle, I have a better knowledge of the inner make-up and daily life of each child/family separate from the school environment. This awareness strengthens our bond, enabling me to take the extra measures, as needed, that might make the difference.

The following entries support how circle affects everyone that is involved:

"In circle, it helps me to tell how I feel inside my heart. I like circle because it makes me a better person. Circle is a time when you say what your true feelings are (like sad, happy, mad, excited, angry, and frustrated). You shouldn't be too shy to say what's in your heart because you have to say what is happening inside of you. You can say what you did on the weekend, a holiday, or what happened at school. Circle is great, wonderful, and so fantastic! It is part of my daily life. When I grow up I will teach circle to everyone." (Melissa, age 10)

"When I first came to a circle, to me it was a foreign and crazy idea. I was nervous when we first all sat down to share our feelings. It was new to me then, but now I know how much it affects my life. As I look back on circle, I sometimes think about some of those continuous loops, and people arguing back and forth. However, almost every circle, people were able to get rid of bad feelings and tough stuff.

Today, because of circle, I know how to talk out problems with my friends. In my new school, we don't have it, and sometimes I need it and really miss circle. Even though I look back and realize how much time it took sometimes, it helped (and still helps) me with my conflicts. Circle taught me how to handle them on my own too. It certainly was magical for me." (Heather, age 12)

"I think circle has helped my son Cory develop his latent compassion. Although it may not show overtly, he has lots of empathy. For instance, his soccer coaches would go crazy because every time a kid got hurt on the field, regardless of the team he was on, Cory would stop playing and run over to help the child. Now, through circle, he is becoming aware of pain that is not always so obvious, when a child's feelings are hurt. He is learning a lot about life.

Everything seems to flow and my children thrive in a happy, positive classroom. My son and daughter are appropriately challenged in the same multi-aged class. Interestingly, as siblings, they have never fought in class—they just treat each other as another student. Because of circle and feeling good, children are able to accept each other more easily. When kids are pulled out of class for various reasons—specialists, academic help, speech, meds—the other kids don't even blink.

Circle has helped me in many ways. I understand the kids at school much better, as it gives me glimpses into their more private feelings. It has helped me socially, in that I've learned to express concerns in a non-threatening way. To be able to say "I have a concern about . . ." versus directly "attacking," such as "Why are you doing . . ." expresses the problem in a way that does not automatically engender a defensive attitude." (Brenda Yoshinaga, parent)

A freshman college student appeared one day and asked if she could observe, visit, or volunteer. This young woman came back year after year throughout her college education. It was rewarding to be her master teacher and mentor as she student-taught under my guidance. How sad and joyful when the year ended; it wasn't really a "good-bye," but a beginning of her role as a graduate and an educator:

"The first day I visited Gail's classroom, I experienced circle. At first I felt uncomfortable, invited to sit on the floor amongst small children.

But when I realized how serious the children took circle time, how important it was to them, the discomfort vanished. Circle is a time when kids can get together as a class and discuss what's bothering them or what's making them happy, all with adult facilitation. That's the key word —facilitation. During circle, the teacher doesn't necessarily lead the discussion, but monitors and helps. Circle is totally child-centered. Having circle in the classroom helps children deal with things that we, as educators and adults, may not find particularly troublesome but to them means the world.

I saw, firsthand, the effect circle can have on the children and classroom environment. When I first sat down to circle, I was an observer. I was volunteering and observing, and circle was part of the day. When I started student teaching in Gail's class, I became an active participant, facilitating and contributing to our circle time and experiencing for myself the power of circle. Then, when I had my own class, I started using circle time. I taught in an inner-city school located in South Central Los Angeles. A school where we weren't allowed to stay past 4:30 p.m. and where there were at least three lockdowns a year. My fourth-graders loved circle —they anticipated it all day. For the first time, they had a voice! They had a safe place to voice their concerns, questions, and appreciations. They learned to talk about their problems rather than act on them.

Now, even though I have moved away from Los Angeles and those children, I still get letters from some of those kids asking me how to talk through problems they're having in school or at home. I truly feel that incorporating circle into my regular school day has given many of the students the skills they need to work through problems rather than resorting to violence. I've seen circle work. I've seen it empower children to make better choices and to treat others better. Circle should be a part of every child's day. If this were the case, maybe our schools would be a safer, more comfortable place for our children to learn." (Laura Walters, teacher)

*Laura Vallejos
(now Laura Walters:
elementary teacher).*

THE SHY ONES: THEY ARE ALWAYS LISTENING —SOMETIMES MORE THAN YOU THINK

The right to pass in circle is important because everyone participates in his or her own way and needs to feel comfortable. Sometimes a participant's contribution is to listen. Silence can send a message when one is examining what is being communicated. An integral part of circle is the continuous support that you are seeking from all students, asking them to do their best!

A parent, Toni Boucher, says:

> Jessica saw and heard from her peers that they too had problems and concerns of their own. That everyone is not perfect and others are just as scared and uncomfortable. Even if she doesn't talk, she listens and learns from others like herself. Her self-esteem has just boomed. She's trying a lot of things that she never did in the past. She's not afraid of making a mistake on paper. So you see she has grown to accept her faults and is not afraid to accept them. Circle shows her interest and enthusiasm. It shows that she does matter and that she is not just another "kid."

I KNEW I HAD COME FULL CIRCLE

Kathy Dawes in first grade.

Kathy Provenzano: special ed. teacher.

I watched the children sit on the floor with her, eagerly awaiting a story she was about to read. Then they busily did hands-on follow-up activities. Ms. Dawes, who was in the process of completing her dual credential in elementary education and special education, was successfully teaching her first lesson. I heard one child tell her, "You will be a good teacher because I especially like the way you read stories and make learning fun. You are just like Ms. Gail." She was herself, a student in my class and has since signed a contract to guide her own special ed. class.

Kathy Dawes says of herself:

As a young child, I vividly remember being shy. When adults spoke to me, I would hide behind my mother or father. I kept to myself and never stirred up trouble in public. I don't remember much about preschool, but what I do remember was being deathly afraid of going and leaving my mother. Everyone figured I was going through one of those "phases." However, when I entered elementary school my shyness and fear remained. I made a few friends, but if they were absent, I would play quietly by myself.

Speaking in front of the class was the worst possible torture one could inflict. I didn't want to stand up in front of the class, but they would make me. I could feel my body temperature rise, my face turn red, and hundreds of eyes glaring at me. They were all waiting for me to make a mistake or say the wrong thing. I was an insecure, awkward beanpole of a young girl. I was consumed with the fear that my insecurities would be discovered.

Fortunately, someone recognized my fears. My first, second, and third grade teacher recognized my insecurities. That's right, I had Ms. Gail for three years and I thank the Lord every day that I did. She didn't change me. She merely showed me how to overcome my fears. She taught me that it was okay to express myself. I remember writing a positive thought daily. What sticks out was the fact that she read what I was writing and made comments. This was so special because it made me feel that what I had to say was important enough for her to read. She was a busy teacher, but she took the time to read what I had to say and give me feedback.

Over time, I learned it was okay to express my opinion to the class. Ms. Gail didn't force me to speak like others had. She simply encouraged me to speak when I was ready. If I wasn't ready to speak, that was okay with her. When I finally contributed, it felt like I was on top of the world. Yeah, I still turned red and my body temperature rose every time I spoke in front of the class, but the point is, I was able to express my own opinion and myself.

These communication skills have gotten me far in life. Many teachers pushed the shy student to speak and praise the self-motivated talkative individuals. She praised each of her students equally and allowed them to grow at their own pace. Occasionally, she'll give those like me a push, but she doesn't make you be anyone you're not ready to be. Students leaving Ms. Gail leave feeling like an individual with an opinion and self-confidence!

From one of the silent ones, Ms. Jenny Mihaly:

Jenny Mihaly in first grade.

I have always been shy and did not care for group discussions. I found it hard to share with others what I was thinking and feeling. I feared I would make a mistake or say the wrong thing. Only after a while was I able to feel relaxed enough to willingly participate. I tended to hold back until I was comfortable with the people around me. Upon reaching that comfort level, I began to feel more confident with myself and my abilities. I was not as afraid to make a mistake, and I began to realize I did not have to be perfect in everything I did.

In school, I was usually ahead of most of my classmates; learning came easily to me and I understood what was going on. I also possessed the determination to do well. I think that because I did not speak in circle very often, my listening skills benefited from it. I could pay attention in class and learn better. I would often pick up on minor details that others would overlook or not remember. My greater capacity to learn made things a bit awkward in my younger years, I had to deal with adversity from my peers at times. You found supplementary books for me to read because I had already read the assigned ones. Although this set me apart from my peers, I am lucky I had this opportunity. Instead of rehashing something I had already read, you helped me discover and delve into something new and expand my creative thinking. My love for reading was satisfied by taking home special books to read on vacations. Being able to feel comfortable enough with myself allowed me to push on and deal with those situations. I refused to compromise myself and give in to the norm. I did not want to let what others thought affect me.

*Jenny Mihaly:
marine biologist.*

Eventually this all passed when I moved on from elementary school. My abilities did not stand out as much because I was surrounded by others who had gone through the same. In high school, doing well in academics led to rewards and college opportunities. My consistent hard work paid off as I was named valedictorian. It wasn't something I strove for; it was just a nice way to commend something I found natural, doing my best.

I am currently attending UCLA and majoring in something I have always had an interest in, marine biology. I have the opportunity now to study and conduct my own experiments at one of the country's top marine laboratories. I look forward to eventually using my knowledge to help safeguard marine mammals and their habitat. Being comfortable with yourself and your abilities can get you very far; you realize your full potential. I believe I have grown a lot from the person who was afraid to open up to others. With the right guidance and support, I was allowed to be who I was. I never was pushed, or allowed myself to be pushed, into being something I was not. I quietly took in everyone's advice and developed my own path in life. As a result, I feel I have come full circle. A little self-confidence can lead to success and the realization of goals.

Yes, the shy child who appears withdrawn and timid can reap extra benefits from a circle experience. The choice is theirs to listen and absorb what others around them are saying. Suddenly, they realize that peers are talking about and dealing with things that they too are wondering about. Each circle adds a layer of security that we are all human. The comfort zone is there to hear things one never thought others felt or were concerned about. And one day, this is the child that opens up to share with others. To finally be able express what has been inside, and for peers to not only listen but also accept, smile, and understand. And when that day comes, that child feels reluctant at first, then relieved, and jubilant!

ADDENDUM

The morning after I completed this chapter, a novel experience confirmed once again that no two circles are ever the same. The fifth day of this new school year the students followed me to find a tree with shade. I was impressed that they already knew the format of circle as they looked up to me to begin. So I did, "We will share many surprises and unusual moments this year. We need to be flexible and united. I appreciate how unique and special each of you are. I just thought we'd sit comfortably outside, hear the rustle of the wind in the trees and the sound of birds singing." They all quietly listened . . . as three birds dumped on three children—on one's head, on one's shoulder, and on one's back. We all looked at each other and quickly moved to a nearby grassy area. With harmonious laughter, in unison we said, "We appreciate that those birds didn't get all of us!"

Circle

I used to care most about toys and things. Now I chose to care about my friends who all care about me.

Circle is making people more comfortable!

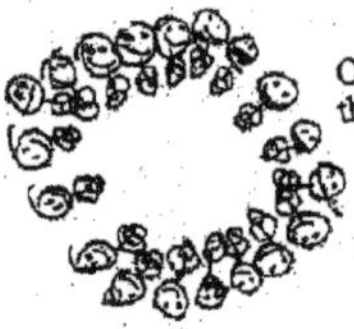

One person may feel alone and they can say that they are lonely and need a friend or pal.

It is helping me to start thinking about things I do.

Circle

It really helps me express myself and deal with my problems. If you had someone help you, you can also appreciation that!

I like circle because it makes me feel closer to other people.

Circle is a special part of the day.

Bird's eye view of circle

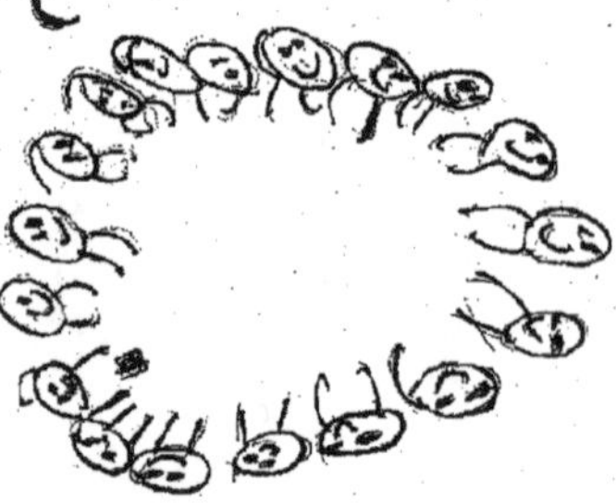

Circle

I was always in trowble - not any more.

Sometimes just listening in circle helps me feel inside and makes me feel better.

Circle helps me. I am becoming a better person!

Circle

I had a special place to talk and special people to listen.

Circle allows me to express my sadness or happiness.

We Get along.

One day I used my words to help someone who couldn't express herself. We all just looked at each other and it was like magic!

Why doesn't everyone have a circle?

Just the other day I found out how I mistreated others and I didn't even know I had done such a thing. So I learn and that makes me happy.

We use two big words. We use appreciati' ones and Concerns. We are all more considerate and are very much aware. We are very understanding and value each other!!!

If someone is down we can help them feel better.

I can always say what I think no matter what it is.

CIRCLE

Don't you think everyone should have a circle?

I was happy too.

When I'm in Circle, I feel special!

sad but happy

I can express my feelings to anyone about anything. We all can. Sure wish everyone around the world could! communicating.

circle is

Now-I can't wait to hear what everyone says, including me!

by leting Circle helps me feelings. me reveal my

It helps people know each other. We solve our problems and get along better. That makes everyone happy!

I got rid of fights and frustrations. Now I can solve my problems better. My days all became happier!

7

THE ORGANIZATION

Training students to be organized helps everything become easier for students, parents, and teachers. This begins with one expectation at a time (an hour, perhaps, or a small time block) and gradually develops into the bigger picture. Techniques and strategies can and should be adjusted to meet the needs of all students (and educators).

Courtney

Stating your projection clearly lays a solid foundation, indicating your purpose, goals, and objectives. Students and families informed about the course of studies will better understand what you are teaching and "where you are going."

Every day, children bring to school their own worries, problems, thoughts, and lives. Now in college, former student Staci DeLuca says,

I remember how scared I was to be in school. Especially, when a new year started. I didn't know what to expect but a teacher could always make it

okay. Showing me that I was able to express myself made me see how interesting learning was. When I took my seat, I was ready and excited to
learn what was in store for the day. If I made a mistake, I began to realize
it was okay. It is something that everyone does and it is a part of life. A
teacher has the ability to get me interested in what I learn so when each
day starts I can start it with a smile.

Establish an inviting, successful climate and demonstrate a positive
attitude (*especially* day one). Challenge them each and every day. Sequential learning helps children acquire skills day by day. Teaching that
adapts to students' needs and interests is done through both oral and
written lessons. Be a role model and teach them to think, to listen. Encourage them to want to listen. You too . . . *listen* . . . to *what* they have
to say. My objective is to instill in every child the desire to learn.

The environment is the place where learning is going on. Foster an
environment that is conducive to learning and is exciting. Fill it with experiences and academic challenges. When students are enticed, the
learning environment becomes a part of them. When students work together, there is continuity along with an apparent blend of expertise, desires, and enthusiasm. Watch their faces as they delve into vast educational opportunities.

As you welcome students, include a variety of comfortable activities
so they will experience mutual support and synergy right from the beginning. Value individual differences. Include networking among all of
the children, as peer validation and class-building experiences. Creating
a positive class identity in which students have a chance to contribute
and get to know each other becomes a cooperative classroom. This dimension transforms teaching goals and a working environment into an
enriching endeavor for all.

A classroom is a working, learning environment and it should be
"home" while the students are there. Those who have been in my classrooms will agree that they are colorful and full of student creations displayed everywhere. Students feel ownership of their classroom. However, underneath the creativity is an underlying organization that is
established and maintained by everyone in the class. Possibly my highest compliments have been when substitutes leave notes saying, "Children are on task and so responsible." "They really didn't need me!" "I
learned a lot from your students." "How did you do this?"

HOW MANY TIMES HAVE I HEARD "THEY CAN'T FOLLOW DIRECTIONS"

Why? Ask yourself, how are you giving the directions? Don't just tell them to follow directions, teach them how! Think through the direction you are going to give and begin with one at a time. (Eventually you might work up to three directions.)

When are you giving the direction? Do you have their attention? Is it for an immediate response? Have you clearly stated your expectation explicitly? What exactly are you asking them to do? Do you really know if they understood your direction? Have you allowed for questions if a direction is not understood? Is it a new direction or one they have heard before? Do you need to model the direction? Can you restate it in another way to be sure all are hearing what you mean to say? Are you sure they have heard you? Sometimes just asking a student to repeat directions will reinforce and answer all of the above.

FROM THE BEGINNING

Start with day one. One step at a time! When students complete your "first day" (first lesson), "spell out" your exact expectations. Giving effective instructions increases student success from the very beginning. No, they can't follow you around the room to give you their papers. Establish a specific place to put their work and demonstrate where it goes before they even do it. I have inexpensive plastic tubs throughout the classroom that are clearly labeled for every skill work assignment. (Actually, students have, on their own, made new labels that are colorful with drawings depicting what goes in each tub. They wanted to be sure the structure is clear, easy, and confusion free.) It becomes easy and quite logical. When you have a routine, you have a cooperative, flowing, learning environment. Step by step through teacher sequencing (and praise), children identify with, understand, and appreciate a "routine." Miraculously, student work is accomplished and it is no longer "lost" nor misplaced.

Responsibility learned at school transfers into the home where everything you do can be reinforced in some way. Instruct children in the strategies of accepting responsibility. Be consistent. Your reinforcement will teach them to build and accept it. To me, loose papers everywhere is nonproductive. Children use "composition books" to write in or I make them one. On the cover of each "book" appears the child's name and the subject. Student work is written in these books and must include the date. When a task is complete, the book is placed in the appropriate tub for teacher recognition and response.

The student's work gets to the right place because they have learned this expectation. As a teacher, a whole set of student work is there for you to evaluate. Even with different levels or assignments of work due to student diversity, common subject matter is together. Engaging in organization is actually appealing to all. Because the work is ongoing in the same book, you as a teacher can easily see the chronological growth and progression. Also, is the work neat and legible? Is there evidence of gradual improvement and challenge, or is review or remediation necessary? Students of any age can watch their own development as they are experiencing it. I can't tell you how they laugh in amazement when they look back after a few months (or a year) and see the difference. Children will acknowledge what they used to do and they get the chance to see for themselves. "That couldn't have been me!" "Did I really do that?" you will often hear them saying. Instead of papers on the path as students exit the school grounds or who knows where at home, parents can observe a child's progress at any time by seeing it accumulated together.

Exploring the growth and changes of an individual student is not only astounding, but also wonderful for the student, parent, and teacher to appreciate. Another bonus is that parent conferences, or related meetings regarding a child, are easier because everything is there in your hands to view together.

SCHEDULES

Another easy organizational technique is to keep your schedule written on the board visible for all to see: not only your day but also the entire week. Though this possibly takes extra planning, they feel responsible, informed, and it is invaluable. Even young children discover that they can see exactly what they are doing. When you are in the practice of keeping a written "forecast" on the board, how lucky you are when a substitute is a necessity. Your routine and organization are already spelled out. The plans you will write are additional and supplementary. (From the first day of school, it is recommended to prepare a folder of basic plans for any day if an emergency does occur. A substitute will have a minute-to-minute guideline with spelled-out lessons that are appropriate, so the day will go smoothly for your students.)

Students like to anticipate and plan in their own minds what steps they are taking in the learning process day by day. I purposely do this before any vacation (usually weekends as well.) It organizes me to have everything ready so I don't have to "think" and can enjoy myself more. In reality, the impact is intended for the children to see that the minute they are back from vacation, they also return to the routine. I find that in this way teaching time is not lost.

Sometimes I have felt certain students (classes) have benefited from a written contract. When this is the case, make it simple. The students can help you name the written document and include them to assist you in designing the list of tasks. Use sequential order so it is easily followed. Include a check-off box or spaces of some sort for students to easily mark completion when a goal is attained. This reinforcement can begin as a daily process and then progress to weekly.

ORGANIZATION OF SEATING

I recommend allowing students to have a choice where they sit. In my class, there is no table one, row three, or designated seating. The "rule" is to sit somewhere different each day. They keep their belongings in cubbies so there is no problem regarding books and personal belongings. Actually, cubicles are more visible so they are more organized and things don't get stuffed or lost in desks. I find a more cohesive group of peers who get to know their classmates better.

As you set the tone in the beginning of your school year, maybe you would prefer to set standards and rules, going into this gradually. Possibly this could be a goal for students when they are in compliance with your expectations. If this is not for you, try to at least change your students' seating monthly. When students sit in different areas, intermingling varies as does somewhat the class personality. Even discussions seem to take on a new dimension with participation coming from different places in the "new" composition.

Approximately four times a year, when the mood strikes, I ask the students to help me to rearrange the entire classroom. They come up with ways that I would never have thought of. They take on new ownership and pride in "their" room. Change is good and we always learn from it. It is almost a new beginning and a new aliveness permeates once again.

AS YOU ORGANIZE

Our responsibility is to remember that no two children are the same and to discover their needs and idiosyncrasies. We must eliminate our own tendencies to prejudge.

My mom was once a teacher and gave me her best advice on my first day of teaching: "Form your own opinions. Get to know your students for who they are. Don't read the words on cumulative records until after winter break. Children grow and change, get to know them in your own eyes."

Recognize a child's character and individuality. The one who gave the last teacher the most trouble may be the shining star when he gets to you. Students grow (outgrow) stages. I remember teachers telling me, "I know your brother." It was okay to be a sister, but our styles, interests, and study habits were different. I felt insignificant because I just wanted to be "me."

Once, as a new school year was about to begin, colleagues laughed at a child's name appearing on my first-grade class list. They shared, "He's already been retained. He is beyond anything you can imagine. Good luck! Hope June comes soon." I embraced him with things that captured his interest along with creativity and praise. I wish I knew where all those teachers are today because I would post a billboard to tell them the news. This "hopeless child" has just been the number-one recruit for universities across the nation!

Once I heard a story of some teachers being told "children's scores." The class was divided into groups accordingly. Later, it was revealed that those scores weren't the IQs at all, but only digits of phone numbers!

FLEXIBILITY

Evaluate, diagnose, continue to reevaluate, and diagnose—as you go. Don't label! Formulate your own feelings about a child's capability. Allow and accept change! Students fall in and out of their "niche" as they grow and develop. Groupings in each subject matter need to be adjusted as children slide in and out of skill levels. Students master concepts at different speeds. Be careful not to put them in a category that can't be altered. It is important to recognize this because students stay motivated with challenge and discipline problems lessen.

INDIVIDUALITY

Don't have preconceived notions because you don't really know something until you experience it.

Two brides, two sisters, yet as different as day and night! I was invited to a double wedding. In my mind, I thought it would be a double ceremony. I never could have anticipated this experience. Two sisters, close in age, similar ideas, and the same family—but it wasn't just a double wedding, because they emphasized individuality and uniqueness. Each gazebo was beautiful with flowers representing the bride's personality and the magnificent gowns depicted their "style" and dreams.

In between ceremonies, all of the guests gathered to share the "moment" and the entire setting changed for the second wedding. The brides had each been students in my class for first, second, and third grade, six consecutive years. Because they didn't want me to feel "old," I was introduced as their mentor in life.

The celebration after included everyone together and an atmosphere of rejoicing. To me, it was a profound message. As a teacher, it brought to light that you don't "know" students until you really know them. It reminded me to guide students, to not prejudge a situation, or to be judgmental of

*Deanna and Krissy Gomez
in their early elementary years.*

others. Teach students to accept people for who they are. We can all learn from others. Guide them to understand that they don't "know" things until they experience them.

I might note that the parents of the brides were parent volunteers in my class for years. The third sister, also very different (as siblings are) now has her daughter in my class. The grandparents have another generation in my class and have even returned to help me.

EVERY CHILD NEEDS YOU

I think the biggest challenge for educators is how to challenge your students, whether they are remedial, gifted, or average.

The remedial students need varied methods, along with teacher patience, to help them to apply themselves so they can take the steps to achieve their accomplishments. (And, how exciting it is when they do!) Some students need more encouragement. Others just need practice in an essential skill to improve and reinforce what they are studying. Aside from academic differences, there are so many levels of life skills such as: maturity, problem solving, organization, follow-through, recall, listening skills, and self-awareness. For those who do need it, it is up to the teacher to find and recommend ways to get support help when it is necessary.

Sometimes I find the most "problem" child exhibits traits that might be that of giftedness. Some examples could be poor attention, boredom, endless questioning, or nonconforming, strong-willed, and other "inappropriate behaviors."

Now a radio DJ, Amber Scott says,

> The most important thing for teachers to remember is that everyone learns at different rates. While more attention is usually put on students who are behind, an equal amount of attention needs to be given to students who are advanced. They feel just as out of place as remedial students. Most teachers assume that they will excel. The fact is that most advanced students feel bored and restless and therefore are more prone to cause trouble. She listened and that was how I met Gail when I was sitting on a bench for time out because my first grade teacher always reprimanded me. I was very inquisitive, asked all sorts of questions, and usually did things my own way. Because I didn't fit into a teacher's

predetermined mold of a "good student," I was branded a troublemaker. The sad thing was, I had no idea why. Now I constantly think things up and continue to create, and be creative and articulate . . . like I always was. Only now I have the freedom to do it—to generate new ideas and new ways of doing things that ultimately improve the station, the music, the ratings, and the listening.

Jim Delisle is an advocate for gifted children. According to Delisle,

> Gifted children think and feel more deeply than others their age. They might not manifest their high intelligence in advanced school perform-ance or exceptional productivity, but they do show their adeptness in other ways—by the questions they ask, the humor they understand, the inequities they uncover, and the logical inconsistencies that are vividly real to them
>
> The most gifted seven-year-old in the world still feels shallow if no one will sit next to her at lunch, and even the biggest eleven-year-old will wince if picked last for a recess kickball team, even if he can rationalize that it matters little in life's bigger picture. They hurt, they bleed, they cry; and when gifted children are dismissed as being just like everyone else, they are bright enough to know this is wrong, but fragile enough to hurt from this insult to their intelligence.
>
> Let us respect gifted children enough that we will acknowledge their abil-ities and insights as a natural part of who they are—not better or worse than anyone else, neither freak nor geek, but merely a member of our diverse hu-man family, "where one size fits all just doesn't fit anymore." (Delisle 2002)

MAKING A DIFFERENCE

Tim was every teacher's dream, but only for three weeks a month. His commendable attitude, peer relations, academics, and everything he did was exceptional. That one week a month, though, he would turn into (excuse me) a monster. It was like clockwork. To me, it seemed like a "movie," a true drama, and unfortunately this went on for most of the school year. As a teacher, it is sometimes necessary to record observa-tions, dialogue in depth, and implement behavior modification. We all tried everything possible, yet to no avail. I often wondered how Tim thought about all of this. It was so simple as the mystery unfolded! It was finally discovered, an allergy! No, not to school or me, but to foods containing nitrates. One week a month, Dad would be home for breakfast and it was on those days that Mom prepared a "traditional" family breakfast for the entire family. It consisted of juice, toast, jam, eggs of varied styles and either ham, sausage, or bacon.

A CHILD'S QUESTION: WHY?

If you walked around the world without glasses and you couldn't see, think of all the things that you would miss out on (especially if you were diagnosed for glasses by a well recommended physician!). I know, many feel ADD (ADHD) doesn't exist or is overly diagnosed and we're not supposed to talk about it. However, if a family approaches me on this issue, I give them the analogy of walking around in a fog, without focus. One family continuously discussed the possibility over a two-year span. They "didn't believe in it" and I, as an educator, could not really say. It was their doctor who diagnosed the child, who was reluctantly put on medicine. She was closely monitored, given minimum dosages that were modified as she became more focused, and with no side effects. Alone in my classroom one day, immersed into whatever it was I was doing, this former student came in to tell me what had obviously been on her mind quite awhile. "Can I ask you a really important question?" "Sure" was my answer, as she would have continued to tell me anyway. "Why didn't you, my teacher, or my parents do something sooner? Everything is so easy now. I go to school and all I have to do is to learn. I have control now about things I say and do. I can be myself. This makes everyone around me happier, and especially me!"

CONFIDENTIAL

Students feel good when you have circle because it is a satisfying experience. Establish a safe environment in your class or circle that is conducive to students opening up while maintaining confidentiality. As you create an empathic role, you are helping them to feel understood. Not only do problems continuously diminish but also children grasp the tools to communicate throughout their life experiences (good and bad).

Once a usually gregarious, fun-loving student was overly sensitive, withdrawn, and moody all day. When I asked him why, "Nothing" was the quick, short response. Now we are all entitled to bad days and we all know that. Somehow though, our eye contact told me there was something more. (Watch for their subtle differences and be attuned to "signs" and changes.) When everyone was gone at the end of the day, he lingered to say, "You'd be in a bad mood too if" and he lifted his shirt to show me what looked like stripes across his entire back. They were boot marks where his dad had kicked him over and over again. My heart went out to him and I've come to realize that nothing amazes me.

I wrestled with myself about the report yet I knew I had to do it. It was because of my personal shortcoming and my fondness for this child that I had difficulty facing the family after that. The configuration of the family changed gradually as help was attained. This story, difficult to believe, had a happy ending. Through therapy and help, the family was put back together again. I just recently heard that the boy, now grown, is thriving. So, deep down, I know I did the right thing.

It is inconceivable what judges in our courts have seen and heard. Retired Los Angeles Superior Court Commissioner Liewen advises,

As an educator, you are with children more hours of the day than anyone else. You should be familiar with each child's personality, behavior and nuances. If there is a radical, or sometimes even a subtle, change in a child's behavior, school work or demeanor—be on the alert and talk to the child. Not every change signals abuse, but many can. If you have any inkling that abuse, emotional or physical, has taken place, file your report. In California, teachers, among other professionals, are mandated reporters. Please don't take it upon yourself to investigate and make a determination of abuse. Let the social workers, physicians, attorneys and judiciary make that decision. The report you don't make or delay making, could develop into life-long physical or psychological trauma or even the death of a child. And, don't think that your neighborhood is exempt. Abuse is not just the province of minorities or lower socio-economic areas. It happens in all walks of life and crosses all ethnic and socio-economic barriers. (Liewen 2002)

As a teacher, listen. Give your support and be there for your "children." I have worked for several administrators throughout my career. One filed papers without reluctance on any suspected "possibility." I respect her discretion because cases (realities) beyond my least suspicion were uncovered and have been real. I know we as educators are afraid to get involved, and some accusations are indeed unfounded. You can't take a chance with a child because you are not the judge. Don't try to interpret or justify suspicions. We're talking about children who are powerless human beings; many who feel abandoned, guilty, and worthless. Some think their "treatment" is the norm or must continue as a means to be "loved." If called on to testify, it is our obligation to be an advocate for a child, to help to protect children who can't protect themselves. Making a difference can get a student out of a situation of abuse, neglect, abandonment, and/or drugs. If something is indeed happening, you are positively affecting a child's entire future. You as the teacher are influencing a student's outlook, including the psychological make-up and view of self.

Some families are in denial, not wanting to believe or acknowledge what is going on within the walls of their own homes. A parent doesn't believe it, or doesn't want to believe it. One adult might cover for another, afraid of the ramifications involving the system or their "loved" one. There is a power of adults over children and also, a child might be threatened not to tell. "I'll kill you or your mom if you tell. It's all your fault anyway." Sexual abuse and beating can be done by family, extended family, a babysitter, childcare provider, or anyone. Who even knows? Hurt and abuse can be of the mind, not just infliction of the body.

This isn't a topic I wanted to address, but we need to! Though children often are not the best communicators, listen to what they are saying (and to what they are not saying). As a teacher, get to know your students. They are with you how many hours of every day? You should be familiar and recognize signals or changes in behavior patterns, work, study habits, and communication. You can see it in their faces, their eyes. You can see the look of fear, shame, distance, preoccupation, or being lost in another world. This is another reason to build trust, mutual respect, and confidence.

Each year, there is usually one child in my class who goes through a clearly identifiable "problem." How I try to block out the "details" of the students over the years that have been suffering, neglected, abused, or molested. Sometimes I have to wonder, if I have seen so many cases over the years, what about all of the children everywhere that don't "communicate?" Not only do they keep everything in, but whatever it is that is happening in that child's life is often repeated over and over. Listen to what the children tell you. Report anything you suspect as threatening or a wrongdoing. Though it takes time and is not on the top of the list of things you want to do, you might save or change a life (or lives).

One of my students once spoke openly to a judge about being molested. The family told me that they felt this was made possible because of the tools learned in circle. With a stuffed animal safely in hand, the child was asked what she was feeling inside and felt genuinely relieved when the testimony was done. No, the wrongdoing can't be undone, but with help the child can go forward. Speaking to the court, the child said, "I hope you can do something now. If not, there are other children this may happen to." Words about details of what had happened were expressed with "and I hope that it won't happen to other children out there."

8

WHEN IN DOUBT, ASK THEM TO TAKE A SURVEY

Courtney

Education should be like a shoe, a favorite shoe. The learning process should be comfortable (not too tight and not too loose—just right). In a comfortable atmosphere, students can put their thoughts and energy into learning as much as you will teach them.

Teachers and parents should attempt to "walk in their shoes." How does a child feel? What kind of "steps" are they taking? Too fast? Too slow? Vigorous stride? Slow gait? Be aware of their manner of pace, the movement students exhibit, and the distance that is covered. Can you as an educator add an extra bounce to your students' each and every step?

Through experience, they can engage in remarkable topics and processes with endless possibilities. Give them an idea firsthand as a guide and engage your students in the process. Once you jump-start their minds, they will investigate and obtain data that you might have never even thought about.

Speaking of shoes, now that is a favorite project of mine! (Especially on the first day, or to culminate the first week.) For a meaningful and different writing sample, ask the students to use written language to describe the shoes that they are wearing (depending on the level of the students—young ones can draw great pictures and/or dictate).

Encourage them to make a list of attributes or to draw a web to outline their thoughts. Get them to begin describing a few ideas and let them go from there. You will learn much more about your students' abilities because this is not the usual question ("What did you do this summer?"). With good humor, you are already warming up to your new class of students. You are asking them to do something valuable for you for diagnostic purposes, while also giving an indication that you have a personality and this year is going to be a special one.

Now do you really think any other teacher has asked them to do such an activity? This process will be insightful for the children because they will be recording ideas and data of choice. Take this further, of course! Discuss what mathematical analyses your students might be able to do. How many have tie shoes, velcro, buckles, slip on? What about colors— brown, black, white, tan, or other? And there is always the shoe size, as well as the actual measurement of their foot in inches and/or metric units.

You have now initiated an involved class discussion using a common topic among a group of strangers. I have found this successfully applicable with any age child, as well as adults! Through this type of process, your audience becomes amused, curious, uninhibited, and actually eager to participate. With such a valuable writing sample and active group interaction, you will need to stop and take a break.

You have already allured your students to begin thinking independently. They are also now on the road to becoming challenged to seek their own curiosities and data. How exciting when students not only start to recognize likes and differences but become insightful to begin seeking analyses of their own choice.

It is after the break that the real fun (and learning) truly begins. This is when you greet them at the door with only one shoe on! Yes, and you also ask them to each remove one shoe and place it in a designated spot. Picture the diverse variety as the classroom environment becomes collective, visual, and humorous, and how enthralled the students will be.

Conversation becomes nonstop and students interact together to share a community purpose, to find infinite possibilities, and to share substantial facts.

This will be a whole-group activity that spins into small-group collective work. Students will search for questions, and discover organizational techniques and various methods to identify the facts that they are seeking. Shoes can be sorted in innumerable ways. The interesting math graphs that evolve can be placed on the wall for students to take ownership in while decorating the learning environment. The beautiful part of such an experience is that the students are not only getting to know each other but also working together with direction and determination. Substantial learning will continue, combined with the climate of a cohesive group of students.

Your classroom will be interesting enough for students to encourage others to come to see what they have developed. A great positive way to get parents to peek in too. Why wait until conferences or Open House to meet and dialogue? This is real learning and vitality in the classroom.

Now did I say this is an opening activity? Yes, and one that can continue to evolve (and it will). Compare findings with students in another classroom, or in families or neighbors? Compare foot/shoe sizes with favorite characters in storybooks. What about an elf? Giant? Favorite athlete? Investigate the vast spectrum of books in the library that involve fairytales or stories involving feet and footsteps. Have you taken your students to the school library or on a field trip to the local community library? Help them obtain library skills now to better familiarize them with how to locate books, while also expanding their thirst for learning.

Surveys become a way of life. Math possibilities in graphing are accomplished and understood. Children take genuine pride in organizing these various explorations that always continue to open new avenues in learning. Direct students to compare their unique findings and survey results mathematically. Have them find the likes and differences in data. Some students truly get so involved. Do they really know that they are developing essential life skills? Counting? Comparing? Recording? Reading? Labeling? Interpreting? Different kinds of graphs? They can't wait to discover more!

Promote the elements of interviewing as you encourage children to investigate and run an analysis of their given topics. It's never too early to introduce note-taking skills, which transfer into written results, comments, and reports. Colorful illustrations and posters can further add a visual component that often evolves into oral language, public speaking, and presentations.

These survey activities encourage students to believe in themselves. When asked to do a report or one of these "surveys," the response is always, of course! They have so much to find, to say, to write, and to share. Peers acknowledge each other's accomplishments that produce stronger confidence regardless of the student's actual level of performance, as long as they have done their best.

What about the class newspaper you can now write to further the findings, writing skills, editing skills, and appreciation for each other's special qualities and contributions? This, especially, has promise because an important, essential task will be for all to collaborate and produce a "newspaper" or possibly a news broadcasting video, depending on the age of the students. Diverse interests and desire will ultimately include team meetings and a united effort to devise specific tasks, such as someone to design the title and format, and others to write, edit, illustrate, type, feed into the computer, compile, distribute, and so on. Don't forget to include the weather here, there, and everywhere, and to promote further creative topics that can be coordinated into the group project.

A fun game is to initiate conversation and a new topic when you ask a few individuals to just stand up. Let the students figure out what characteristics you are looking for. Teach them the process of elimination as all are experiencing this positive learning which is now so much fun. Students become so involved that they see it is okay to be wrong and it is fascinating to all who participate. Maybe today, ask five students to stand up. Your class will have to figure out who will sit down. What attributes will they need to focus on? Can they understand the process of elimination? Is it stripes? Number of eyelets on those shoes? Color of hair? Eyes? Or the students' first names (last names?) alphabetically? It can be anything you want it to be! With maturity, it is powerful to select students to take turns leading this favorable learning experience, while at the same time having fun and gaining composure speaking in front of a group.

One day later in the year, you might want to try something different. Should we call it an awareness test? Ask the students to use descriptive adjectives and write about their shoes (socks) without looking down.

That was funny! (Funnier though, was the day I came with my two shoes—same colors, different styles.)

Homework assignments can vary while still fulfilling the purpose of reinforcing skills already introduced in the classroom. Basic math discovery can encourage family dialogue, participation, and discovery. Once for a math extension activity, the children were asked to sort socks at home. You can't possibly imagine the vast variation in graphs and written findings that were turned in.

One little girl always wears two different socks. (Why not? Easy? Different!) A colleague who occasionally is in my class had noticed and questioned this. Funny, that same colleague was on an airplane back East when she recognized this very student on the airplane. The girl with the two colored socks! Mistake? No! An individual? Yes!

Almost any topic in any curriculum can be surveyed. Surveys can take place in the classroom, around the school, in homes, with siblings, family members, the neighborhood, and actually anywhere creative—with teacher and parental approval. How many presidents? Strengths? Weaknesses? Background? What about the states? Comparisons? The weather around the world? What are the contents of children's lunches? What about backpacks? (Color? Weight? Number of pockets? Zippers?) Favorite pets? Birthplaces of family members?

A favorite survey was when we were studying, of all things, totem poles. Each child made a totem pole as a homework assignment. They were displayed with pride in our classroom. Need I tell you? Surveys included likes and differences of totem poles. (Height, width, colors, significance? markings? comparative qualities?)

COLLABORATIVE TEAMWORK—SURVEY

The most simple, inexpensive, different, attention-getting lesson is the day you bring rolls of toilet paper to complement your lesson plan! Students will complete their work with exceptional vigor. After all, how many days do students sit wondering what will transpire with all of those rolls of tp?

Divide your students into teams (of approximately five students) and let the work begin. First, they must collaborate to complete a written assignment giving a description of how to design an original creation (and decide how to wrap a fellow student!). Students will next complete an individual survey: Can they wrap someone up in five minutes? (Without the toilet paper breaking?) How many times will the toilet paper break? Where will they start? How to get the paper off the roll? Thoughts? Suggestions? Recommendations? The teams then compare their surveys and complete a compiled group survey (including a sketch of what the finished design will look like).

Each team must choose who is going to be wrapped. They need to devise a strategy and agree on how they will wrap, including where they will start (toe, head, middle?). The object is to collectively fully dress a teammate using two rolls of toilet paper while being timed for five minutes. If it breaks, they must start over. If the wind blows, good luck or seek shelter. Don't forget to have an impartial judge to make the important decisions! There is no win or lose because this is a team project. Everyone on the team is a winner and a contributor. When the excitement is on, it's difficult for the person being wrapped to stand still. Because if they move, zig or zag, sneeze, or burst out in roaring laughter, how quickly the toilet paper will unravel or rip.

Note: When the project is complete, students need to reevaluate their survey. Did they stay on target? How many times did the toilet paper rip? Did the finished project look like their sketch of anticipation? What would they do differently if they were to do it again?

Cooperation is essential! Shhh . . . I must say the secret is when a team member (or members on either side) hold their fingers in the roll (as in a paper towel holder) so it will unravel with ease!

Before the students go home on this monumental day, have them write a guess of how many squares are on a complete toilet paper roll. Because the next day when they return for math, the squares will be counted to see who calculated the most accurately.

This true test of "teamwork" is ideal after testing or before a holiday! It also elicits group discussion on the importance of teamwork, peer interaction, and having fun.

Homework over the winter holidays? Bows! Students are asked to each bring five bows as the first assignment when they return to school from vacation. This is an immediate and neutral icebreaker after a long holiday break. There is no religious connotation and bows contribute new curiosity, color, and brightness to the new day and new year! Yes, this is like the shoes!

Fulfilling the rigorous demands of the teaching profession can be done. I hope you will insert your own creativity in order to better extend your individual and classroom needs while at the same time fulfilling required curriculum in all subject areas.

9

THEMATIC TEACHING

He came highly recommended for his spunk, his personality, and his ability to get along with others. I was told he was inquisitive yet I heard he was slovenly in his eating habits. I wondered what he'd be like at lunchtime. I thought it was a good idea to bring Teddy to my class to incorporate and coordinate our thematic study. When he walked in the door, the children spontaneously greeted him. He came in with a twinkle in his eyes and smiled at us. I noticed he was a bit reserved, but he gave no hint of the nervousness within. Just like my kids, he looked up to me with such curiosity as the challenge of another best day at school began. In my classroom, you always know to expect the unexpected.

You see, this visitor who came to spend the entire day, was an immense . . . pig! Loud shrilling squeaks could be heard everywhere as Teddy bounded out of my classroom, running throughout an entire school. Teddy, the pig, was on loan to me for one day and what responsibility (fear) I felt as he headed for the main thoroughfare of the city. As hundreds of children were at recess playing on the playground, it was in desperation I involved the help of administrators and colleagues to capture the loose (and very loud) pig. It was a special education child who froze while others ran and shrieked, just like the pig! Suddenly nestling up to the one still child, the pig was calm and also captured! It was at a school assembly that this boy was honored as the hero of the entire school and recognized for his special feat.

Teddy ... the pig!

Unique and innovative thematic learning extends to stimulate all who are lucky enough to be involved. We will long remember the exceptional multilevel stories, illustrations, poems, songs, and tales created that day when students participated in a creative lesson that all began because one child brought a book to school about pigs. Years later, an enlarged portrait of the pig still hangs and sometimes, I hear voices singing the original "Oink" song written that day.

The possibilities of thematic teaching are endless. It began by decorating a large cardboard box with pigs in hopes of finding enough pig stories to fill the box. When the collection grew to over a hundred books, reading became voracious. Data was recorded including writing techniques, vocabulary, story comparisons, character, and setting contrasts. Habitat was studied and discussed.

Math became nonstop too. We made piggy banks using two liter plastic softdrink bottles as the base. Piggy banks took on distinct personalities, with colorful pig faces, feet, and tails—some curly and some unique! At school we filled them with pennies for a school-wide "penny drive" for books that were distributed to 500 students. When the piggy banks went home, students continued to count money and better understand monetary equivalents. Pig money was designed and circulated with different denominations to coincide with our money curriculum. Menus originated, including prices and descriptions of what would be served if we had a "pig" restaurant.

The room environment became filled with large butcher paper drawings of every size and shape of pigs (and wolves!). These were stuffed for a three-dimensional effect. Not only was the room a sight to see but also the dimensions of the creations were measured, recorded, and compared. Classes of all ages throughout the school came to hear original pig stories and academic presentations.

I don't know if I should share this part, but it is true: For "homework," I asked parents to take a picture of their child's room at home. We hung them in amusement! I clearly remember that creative writing lesson did not come close to even thinking about needing a thesaurus! I am told that those children actually cleaned their rooms. The parents stated that "Pig Sty" should be a mandatory lesson required by every teacher, everywhere!

For your enjoyment, our original "Oink" song, to the tune of "Bingo":

"Teddy the pig came to school one day—o i n k o,
We loved Teddy half that day—o i n k o,
Until that pig, he ran away—o i n k o,
The pig went wild, the children screamed, Ms. Gail ran, it was like a dream,
Teddy the pig came to school one day—o i n k o,
We all laughed and almost cried—o i n k o,
Thank goodness the pig he couldn't hide—o i n k o,
In a cage he went the rest of the day—o i n k o,
If you saw this in a movie you'd say no way!!! O i n k o."

Any subject you teach can be maximized to reach fuller learning potential. For example, you can start with a mere weather forecast and springboard it into lessons involving science, geography, culture, and multisubject studies. I could devote an entire book to illustrate the power and potential of thematic teaching. There are infinite ways to stretch any subject or range. I have never used a theme twice, and each new one astounds me at what students can achieve in every academic area. Plus, their inquisitive minds work nonstop to capture learning at its best.

How many steps are there in the Statue of Liberty? Ask your students to research facts and find out! (And the answer is . . . 168.) From this, students calculated how to go up by twos, how many steps are half way, and many other open-ended questions. Extending knowledge and number association, they also discovered that an adult takes approximately 2000 steps to walk a mile. (Curiosity, comparisons, and questions from this can be nonstop.)

Stepping out of "the box" is okay because students are inspired and rise to greater heights. Thematic teaching is an experience involving all levels of learning for every student. Realistically, every class is multi-aged because children bring so many different levels and experiences. It incorporates the "whole" curriculum you present to your students. Thematic teaching is a technique to meet individual and whole-group needs and levels. Integrated components direct learners to engage in supportive experiences providing skill extension and mastery. Challenging continuum parallels teaching objectives to reach competence as children learn through a process in which all subjects intertwine.

Artist Kelly Driscoll recalls:

One day we made pancakes and learned by measuring the ingredients, quadrupling the recipe to make enough for the entire class. There was a boy in our class whose grandfather could never come to school for the fact that he was in the CIA. This day Grandpa came! He was dressed in a cooking apron, equipped with the biggest pancake flipper we had ever seen. With a powerful heave, he catapulted the pancakes into the air to flip them; we guessed the height they soared to. Next, we counted the pancakes and the number we each ate. We measured the results with popsicle sticks, each one equaling each quickly devoured pancake. We analyzed the different sizes and shapes of the pancakes and correlated the uniqueness to our idiosyncrasies. We compiled all of our pancake thoughts into personal pancake books made out of aluminum foil representing the tin frying pan, and decorated with hand-drawn pictures of our festivities. Through this thematic lesson, we learned how to process and categorize data. Every time we thought our lesson was completed, we were struck with a new brainstorm, which would create continuing learning and fun!

Natural curiosity unlocks creativity, which evokes elevated interests. Students transfer their knowledge to better understand through real-life teaching. When you build on a concept, the connecting of multisubjects expands focus and opportunities. A topic that runs through an entire framework is fascinating and stimulating. The results show mandated criteria designed for subject matter is not only met but students want to go beyond. Teachers provide materials and opportunities so that learning is concentrated, shared, and enjoyable.

In all subject matter, curriculum is highly extensive and forever evolving. Math unfolds graphs while science incorporates geographical posters. Spelling and vocabulary are derived from literature representing varied levels, while encouraging fascinating stories and history as well. Letter writing, poetry, and creative writing become part of the process, as do original movies and puppet shows. In thematic teaching, students experience an amazing intellectual stretch as ideas and projects begin to take shape. It is a way to turn on the dynamos, daydreamers, and nonconforming children by creating fun, interesting, and memorable methods. Academic excellence is everywhere!

Mandated goals and standards are not only met but become the seeds from which to grow. Involved children are independent, engaged, creative, and curious in their thoughts. Students constantly display ownership in thematic learning. For example, students were struggling to understand the concept of perimeter. It was through discussions, visual diagrams, and hands-on manipulatives that mastery became evident. Before I knew it, students were researching the dimensions of the new Staples Center. A small group collectively calculated, transcribed, and recorded data onto giant posters. Others sought stats of our Los Angeles Lakers, creating charts depicting basketball scores, individual players' standings, and team comparisons. They figured roundtrip mileage, time from our school, and the creative dream of a field trip there!

Former student Mrs. Isom:

I believe in an atmosphere where the creative bunch have no inhibitions about writing, they just do it and love it and grow their imagination through it. Now that is how I remember your class. I see so many talented students (including my own) that struggle when they don't have a clear picture of their power. When we are able to tear down these walls of fear, that of course is self-induced, they flourish.

HOW TO DEFINE THEMATIC TEACHING

Helene Acton, an instructional assistant in my classroom from 1977 to 1982, developed enriching confidence in my students. She explained the attributes and flow of thematic teaching:

I knew Gail was "cut from a different cloth" when the first question she asked me during an interview was "Are you flexible?" Flexibility in terms of looking at each child's needs is a key component of Gail's teaching. Creativity and enthusiasm permeate every facet of her teaching.

For example, to supplement the reading and cultural program in her multigrade classroom, one year I was asked to help the children to write a French play (capitalizing on French, my native tongue). We wrote a scene about tourists in a French café. The students learned a French song, how to count in French, and chose French names. We ended the unit preparing a French meal. (Throughout the years, many countries were studied, and often included the national anthem, traditional dances, and the production of original plays to present to the families and school).

Sometimes Gail would find a story and had students choose parts to act out. All of these experiences were incorporated into the regular classroom schedule along with math, spelling, science, languages, and other academics. This was made possible in part because of the encouragement of parents to participate in the classroom and capitalizing on their special skills.

It always amazed me how varied activities were going on in the room, students were focused on different tasks, and complete control was kept in the classroom. The beauty of all this was that the children developed a love of learning and each child was motivated at his or her level. Learning was not just a passive activity but an active one in which each child had a special role to play.

Gail has a gift for encouraging children to communicate, for finding a child's particular strength, and for encouraging that child to develop and share it with others, thus building his or her self-esteem. Because of her dedication, her love of children, and her "creative innovative soul," learning is fun and exciting for every child while always instilling the desire to excel.

GET YOUR PASSPORT READY!

"You are about to embark on an exciting and educational cruise around the world! Our ship will make stops on six continents and visit many countries, each a favorite of a particular passenger. Maps will be available soon, highlighting every exciting destination on our itinerary." This is your beginning letter to students to celebrate learning in your classroom. It is great for any age, the older the better! The project should be meaningful and interesting (not frustrating), so tailor the project to individual interests and abilities.

Instruct students to pick a country for your world studies. First, the geography element needs to be addressed. Give a date for maps to be displayed to arouse curiosity of the adventures you are about to discover. Next, research should involve quality library time. Help or assign students to use the library to do research using varied reference materials. Give tips on research techniques, how to make note cards, and how to relate the research along with artifacts, currency, and items of interest to be acquired. Suggest facts to research: flag, music, customs, language, climate, neighboring countries, interesting legends, population, famous people, industry, government, native dress, holidays, exports, education, currency, foods, and . . . more.

Besides written, other possibilities might include an oral presentation or a factual display (three pieces of poster board assembled together can stand to summarize a country with pictures, words, and artifacts) or a mannequin. Use a broom or a mop and secure the stick part securely in a can so it will stand upright on its own. Create a "person" making the head from a broom or mop. Using creative (scrap) materials, dress the mannequin so it becomes a life-size "person" representing your country.

History reports are a slow process, but the end result is a student understanding a country, its culture, and more about this vast world that we live in. An excellent group project is to map out your "voyage," country by country, so students will develop an appreciation and understanding of geography. If students record facts symbolizing information about countries presented, they can refer to their notes and know about many countries, not just their research project.

Mannequins stood in my classroom and were a realistic representation of people and countries around the world. They were dressed in authentic costumes and stood tall and proud. It was like United Nations when visitors entered the classroom. (This is great for Open House.)

Unexpectedly one day, an alarm sounded. I instructed everyone to stop what they were doing. I distinctly told all students to "drop!" They did and safely covered their bodies with their hands, except for one child on my right. "Get down!" I said as I went to take a hand and guide this child in the midst of an emergency. It was a most embarrassing moment, however: the "child" was one of the mannequins, standing tall, well reinforced in the tin can that held it, and hardly able to "get down!"

Depending on time, student age, and inclination, you can take history further:

Treasure Maps—plot them; use different graph styles.

Treasure Chests—we made them out of tomato cartons and filled them with valuable geography words.

Passports—Study authentic ones; design original ones; stamp them indicating finished work.

Travel—Posters/descriptive travel journals, cruise brochures; this assignment can incorporate all academic skills

Letters—Real or make-believe about life in other countries; international pen pals.

Cruise Staff Application—To what ports would you most like (not like) to sail? Using a positive element: Why should you be considered? Attributes?

International Festival—Collect recipes to measure/cook/taste international delights.

Math comparisons: Display and compare international money (colorful bills, differently sized coins, contrast of values and equivalents); how do you compare miles and nautical miles to calculate distances? Given the measurements of a specific ship, what dimensions of your campus compare? With rulers, students measured our entire school in relation to a sailboat, small vessel and a cruise ship. They also figured how many flights of stairs to get to certain places as ascertained from learning to read diagrams/maps of ships.

Thematic Teaching ties it all together. This was a favorite of mine that not only incorporates every academic subject; it also includes 100 percent participation (even those students who never get involved). In the end, some cluster groups even wrote music and put words to it. We sang of countries, knots, treasures, and discoveries of the world.

10

"I HAVE NOTHING TO DO!"

Teach the children to be individuals and to bring forth from within. Things can be simple but they can't and shouldn't be ordinary. I tell my students, "Who knows the possibilities when you open yourself up to others?" Some students have never been asked to give of themselves. Teach them to feel the impact and enjoyment of giving to others (without any expectation). My students grow to know how little things can make such a difference. Sending someone a special note or card might only take a few minutes but it can make a big difference in someone's day, to feel appreciated and that element of surprise! (It's even better, when there is no special occasion!)

GIVING TO OTHERS EXEMPLIFIES A GIFT OF LIFE

Loretta is an adult who observed my classroom and later participated when her youngest child became a student of mine. She even entered the world of education and made it her career. She gave to "my" children her vivacious enthusiasm with a devotion to make thematic experiences come alive. (She is best remembered for her giggle and cooking lessons, guided research, history, and the day we all danced international dances as a culmination, which got media attention.) Her tragedy occurred on a bicycle ride years later, when her bike merely bumped over a pebble. Unfortunately, she hit her head and went into a coma for an extended period of time. My students by that time were not directly connected with Loretta, yet under my guidance they had grasped the concept of reaching out to others.

It Started When Someone Said "I Have Nothing to Do"

Letter from the family:

Loretta is a warm and loving wife, mother, and grandmother. Through the help and motivation of Ms.Gail, she was a parent helper and became a teacher's aide, a job she thoroughly loved. On August 23, 1988, the Miller family's daily routine came to a halt as Loretta had an accident that almost took her life. Instead, she was left with severe head injuries and comatose.

Loretta Miller

During such a crisis, it is vitally important to the person, their family members, and caregivers to have the support and encouragement of friends and well-wishers. Realizing how important this is, Gail made time in her busy teaching schedule for her students to draw lovely pictures, each with an individual get-well message written out to Loretta. She would stop by to deliver the wonderful notes of hope and innocent acceptance of a positive outcome. She decorated our home with murals of brilliant colors and designs. It is impossible not to come out of one's own despair when reading through so many positive thoughts and looking at the wonderful artwork that is unique to children. A person simply has to smile. Imagine that hush-hush household pouring through special notes, enjoying the colors and imagination of each, holding each one up to show Loretta, and watching as her eyes brighten, roaming over each detail.

Imagine each visitor sharing in the household's enjoyment of each note and decoration, adding their comments and encouragement.

It is often the small, thoughtful things that people do that mean the most. With children, those same small, thoughtful deeds take on new significance. The good they do provides hope, joy, and a sense of peace and harmony. They are the future.

Give your students a firsthand lesson about the satisfaction that comes from doing for others. (Many people are not taught this!) When students see the effect of what a small gesture can do, it is not only empowering but they are more apt to do it again. (When you give, you often get back twice as much!) In a "nothing to do" moment, students can write a note, a poem, or make an artistic creation. They will be doing something thoughtful that has no cost yet can bring so much happiness to others. Teaching sensitivity to students, to give of themselves, has a positive affect on society.

When students deliver their thoughtful gift, they are making someone's ordinary day into a special one. The delivery is fulfilling to see someone's face light up from an unexpected (for no reason at all) thoughtful gesture. It becomes contagious because when you make someone else's day, they might spread it further, so a chain reaction begins. Imagine the class discussions and stories something so meaningful can generate! Everyone likes to be appreciated and the feelings received by giving are long remembered. Children usually incorporate this into their daily life. Sharing brings people closer. An intangible bond affecting kids spreads not only an awareness but an opportunity to incorporate positive attitudes into the learning environment.

Suggestions: Keep a "list" in view for some "don't know what to do" moments. Include names of individuals on staff who make a difference, though are possibly behind the scenes and not often acknowledged. Include other possibilities: Local retirement homes and hospitals, veterans or servicemen (how meaningful it was for young children to make cards and notes to send soldiers on Valentines Day!). Have students pick the name of another student and make a positive list, letter, or collage about that person. Give a writing assignment about positive things they have done that have made a difference. (Prior to this, students should make a list of actions and reactions.)

It is powerful for students to discover how gratifying it is to share their spirit with others. Incorporating this quality into your students generates valuable, positive eye-opening, forever-evolving learning experiences.

I have to tell you that it was difficult for me to go to the Miller home because she just lay there. The doctors thought color and chatter would stimulate the patient, yet it all seemed so overwhelming. I brought cheer to a family that sat in the silence of sadness and unknown. I never went with the thought that I could really make a difference, though I believed there is always hope.

Somehow, Loretta Miller came out of her coma. The triumphant moment when her eyes opened! I felt the joys of humanity and love that day. Months later, it was exciting to be able to actually talk to Loretta on the telephone. How ironic that she was now inquiring about me because my voice was raspy and she was intuitive enough to notice. How things do turn around!

Time passed, and the day came for Loretta's daughter, Terri, to get married. It seemed like only a fairytale. As the bride, my former student, and each bridesmaid walked down the aisle, they handed Loretta a beautiful rose. She grasped those white roses in a hand held bouquet while I (and everyone there) wept in the pure magnificence of the moment.

INGENUITY FOR ANY AGE

Write a postcard: those "nothing to do" minutes can be channeled into using time productively. It can start as young as kindergarten; encouraging them to express themselves on paper. They can just draw anything they are thinking or feeling. Record their dictation, which is usually interesting and different. Often, these are treasures you want every parent to see. A postcard format becomes an appropriate, brief means of recording work. On one side is an original drawing and the other, a dictation or self-directed writing. Postcards can go home weekly to the families, except for some that the children might chose to display on a wall for all to see.

Include instruction of the skill of properly addressing a letter or postcard. It is part of the English framework, but amazing to me how many students (even older ones) can't do this accurately. This is part of the basic capitalization skill, along with commas and such. (I ask each student to bring in a few stamps and if it is beyond their budget, I do so.) Upon completion of this study, students independently self-address plain postal-type stickers and three envelopes. How many of our students can address something properly that would actually get to them? When I conclude this study, that is the "final": I take the post-cards and letters with me wherever it is that I am adventuring over a holiday/vacation. It doesn't take much time to write a personal thought on a postcard, apply the "self-addressed sticker" and drop it in the mail. However, there is an excitement and a special bond that builds between a student receiving a postcard and the teacher who took the time to send it. Besides, if they get it, the skill was masterly taught and accomplished!

Shhh? Can you keep a secret? That is what you tell your students—everyone loves a little mystery. Each student draws three random self-addressed envelopes from the pile and is not to tell which en-velopes they get. It is their responsibility to fill each envelope and to mail it. Those who are home with "nothing to do" are excited when an envelope arrives. Those out of town anticipate an envelope await-ing them upon their return. Exchanging envelopes is a simple method to build rapport and further the relationships amongst peers. (Students might choose to put in a cartoon, note, poem, stick of gum, or a dried flower.) It is the idea of fulfilling responsibility by remem-bering to fill the envelope and send it. Plus, children will tell you that learning is fun when letters come in the mail addressed to them! When they ask "can we do it again?" it is another reflection of posi-tive learning

To make a postcard: Have them draw a picture on one side of a pa-per or cardstock. On the back: Draw a line down the middle. On the left, thoughts are dictated or written by the student. On the right, chil-dren (when ready) actually write their address, which is a skill to be ac-quired. In the top right-hand corner, students create an original stamp of their choice (sometimes I have placed a real stamp and mailed a masterpiece home).

Other uses for postcards: Accumulate and bind together a student's postcards as an original book. Send it to important people in student's lives.

Older students increase written skills of concise, to-the-point, descriptive writing. Adhere an actual photograph of the student on the picture side.

CHALLENGE

Brian Landun, in international business, says:

> I credit my elementary educators for the way they challenged me as a kid. Although I was average in certain subjects, I was definitely above average in others. I owe them a debt of gratitude for recognizing this and allowing me to excel. I believe the greatest challenge for all educators is identifying students' strengths. I was encouraged to be "me" and this laid a foundation for my self-confidence. I developed skills for impromptu oral speaking and was allowed to do this in front of large groups. I was enlightened as a public speaker. My self-esteem expanded as my ability was showcased through recognition of my potential. Once identified, educators must allow students to increase their learning potential. Otherwise, students can get complacent and bored . . . thus losing their will to learn. Boredom and complacency can eventually kill a student's resolve . . . which is sad.

THERE IS ALWAYS SOMETHING TO DO!

Look up words in a thesaurus/dictionary

Write a story/letter/ speech

Write down an idea to incorporate later

Study the calendar to find sequence/ patterns

Study/compare athletic team scores/standings

Illustrate what you are currently writing

Proofread an already written piece of work

Work on an original script

Use a story starter to direct new creative writing. (Keep a collection of old greeting cards.)

Read a story that you've been wanting to read/ complete.

Quietly practice a storytelling thought that you would like to share/compose

Make a game out of any academic concepts you are teaching.

Write a note to the teacher giving input or suggestions about studies you want to encounter.

NOTHING TO DO? MEMORIZATION = EDUCATIONAL SUCCESS?

A lifetime skill is ideally what we should teach our students. Skills need to go beyond "memorization" because often it is only short term. As a child, I remember being overwhelmed with those spelling lists and parroting words for the perfect scores. In mathematics, I was required to recite facts out loud, over and over. Through memorization, I learned to read but it was in college that I acquired true phonetic sounds and reasons.

A friend shared a story that she doesn't remember anything she memorized. In college, she was required, along with her classmates, to memorize 400 lines of poetry. Each person had to stand up and say the lines without one mistake. If you made a mistake, you had to sit down and try it again another day. A good way to make one hate poetry.

Knowledge practiced with experience becomes meaningful. If there is a connection between real life and what you are teaching, even memorization can become painless. Improvising with something students can participate in and enjoy instills knowledge that lasts beyond memorization. Incorporate discussions into lessons! Help your students to experience a concept, to say it out loud, and to discover a link. When students are stimulated they get involved.

For example, assign students to make a word find for the important words:

- Ethkemrnisohd*practice*cldkememfig
- Lepsjde*makeituseful*lespso
- Shdneol*showthemthepurpose*tlekft

Writing them and trading or playing games with a classmate is fun for any level or skill.

- $1 + 1 = 2$
- $3 \times 4 = 12$
- $\frac{1}{4} + \frac{1}{4} = \frac{1}{2}$

Incorporate the basics into things they can get their hands on (counters, beans, whatever you or they may find to count). Try or make inexpensive games. With marker, write numbers (or words) and they will be counting, adding, playing whenever they can. They will also be absorbing and mastering what you wanted them to learn in the first place!

- $3 + 2 + 8 = ?$
- $1 + ? + 3 = 5$
- $2 \times 3 \times 6 = ?$

"Golf" is easy for any academic area. On plastic golf balls, write the concepts you are teaching. If you are using words, give numbers for value. If your purpose is math combinations, write a range of numbers. (For older students, play a golf game on the board if you find that more appropriate.) Which is more? Less? By how many? Without competition, ask students to compare scores, tally their finds, and analyze the data. Golf can consist of plastic cups for the holes. Little plastic clubs are fine because it is the sport of learning while having fun.

HAVE YOU EVER WONDERED WHAT TO DO THAT DAY BEFORE A VACATION?

I remember once walking through the school cafeteria just before the winter break. I heard sounds all through the cafeteria, "Shhhhhhh . . . she still believes!" It was students, of every grade, protecting me. Because whenever someone asks me "Do you really believe in Santa?," I always answer yes (and I do, the spirit of the holiday)—but it was a had-to-be-there moment to cherish.

The day before a vacation is not the one when you start a new program, chapter, or book. A gift exchange can make any day a holiday and is a tradition in my class. It eliminates students buying you gifts because it is a "white elephant" exchange. They just bring something (or a $2 limit on a gift purchase). Bring a few extras in case someone forgets. The "gift" rules are: (1) Bring a good attitude, this is for enjoyment. No tears . . . this is in lieu of a lesson or test before a holiday, or perhaps the last day of school. (2) The gift should be appropriate for anyone, boy or girl. (3) It must be attractively wrapped—to create excitement. (4) Have them each pick a number, starting with #1.

When gifts are opened, they are placed in front of that child and are not be touched because they are on display for all to see. Students sit in a circle around the presents. (Start with the highest number and go backward) Each time it is a child's turn, they take a present, either from the middle or they can "trade" by taking a present from a classmate. We say three trades per turn and then the participant must take a gift from the middle. When all have a present, have them open them one by one for every participant to watch. (Requirement: "ooouuus and ahhhhhhh-hhhs." Remember, this is all in fun!) After all gifts are opened, go backward with the numbers and play the game all over again, only this time knowing what the gifts are.

At the end divide the room; those who love (like?) their final gift and don't want to trade and those who do not. This latter group can negotiate and trade. The gift they are giving you is 100-percent participation, good sportsmanship, fun in your classroom—and calmness before the storm of a vacation. As you enter into a holiday, you are teaching your students that it is not about the gifts. It is the unselfish gesture of sharing that is a vital lesson.

11

THE TEACHER DID WHAT?

Education can be amazing and pleasurable. When you make learning fun, you are making an impact that will stay with your students for the rest of their lives. They will continue to exhibit a thirst for knowledge, love of learning, and excel in their numerous endeavors throughout a lifetime.

"Call the Fire Department!*"* I yelled as the process of a new possibility in learning began to take place. Research began and scientific theories were sought to determine how to package a raw egg so that it could be dropped intact. Random collaborative student groups were formed that quickly began working together developing strategy and proposals. Soon, parents and people in the community became involved to guide the students toward success in putting their plans into effect.

Interaction between students in peer groups was positive with a common goal. Participation included sharing thoughts, techniques, schemes, and together ascertaining the necessary materials. Students couldn't wait to get to school each day and the talk of the "best" way to preserve an egg was nonstop. Excitement grew daily, as did detailed descriptions and reasoning along with intricate diagrams and labeling. I've never seen students so eager to learn!

The rules were that cooperation was essential and this was all in fun. Anticipation built as the containers holding the eggs were made from anything and everything. They were concoctions indeed, and each assembled with the hope of withstanding an egg drop.

You could hear the hook-and-ladder fire truck coming toward school. Students gathered in the school parking lot to watch the ladder go up, up, up. The unusual containers containing raw eggs were handed up to the firemen who appeared as curious as the rest of us. The variety of wrappings was interesting and amazing as we all watched each one be dropped to the ground. The adult leader in each student group went out to collect the remains. I think they were more excited than all of their students combined. (No one ever told me until years later that the "egg groups" practiced in homes, with mother helpers on the roof!) Some eggs were smashed, others splattered into gooey pieces, and some were still raw, whole and intact!

This experience next elicited curiosity as comparison data began filling logs with words, thoughts, and reactions. Now the question was, which ones worked (or didn't work) and why. Sincere thank-you notes were written to the firemen who dedicated their time to increase educational desire and made this creative instructional experience possible. The end result was the positive energy exhibited as students of different abilities and levels became empowered in the ever-evolving process of discovery and learning.

GREEN EGGS AND HAM

I try not to get involved with "stories" of other teachers or methods. Sometimes, though, I wonder if a little more natural understanding was extended in some situations, would there be a noticeable difference? This is a parent recollection by Josie Redington about another teacher and how it affected her child almost twenty years ago.

As I rushed in for my appointment with my son's first-grade teacher, I wondered what he had done this time that needed another conference! I knew my son was a bright and precocious child, but could not get the teacher to give him extended work. He seemed bored to me. He complained of finishing the work early, so I had asked Mrs. X to give him some extra work. I thought she would give him higher-level work, but instead of getting rewarded for his quick and accurate work, he was assigned more of the same boring work. We seemed at an impasse. What was I going to do?

I was hoping to clear things up at this conference. It seems students had to stand up and say what their favorite breakfast was. Different children got up and stated conventional breakfasts they liked such as pancakes and various packaged cereals. When it was Benji's turn he stood, paused and with just the right timing and inflection in his voice said: "My favorite breakfast is green eggs and ham!"

Apparently, pandemonium hit the classroom with roars of laughter from the children. I myself had a hard time not laughing out loud as she related the story and failed to see why she didn't see the creativity in this first-grade answer!

The other problem she said was that my son was so squirmy and seemed bored, especially whenever she was talking. I almost lost it when she told me that he was bored whenever she was talking. Well, looking back, I wish I had known sooner that he was being made to feel he couldn't do anything right. Teachers need to know that not all children are able to learn in the same manner nor do the same teaching methods work for all students.

The next year, and the year after, he was in Ms. Gail's class, which fostered a healthy outlook in life. He skipped multiple levels in his academics and was tested into the program for gifted children. I am clearly convinced that had this not happened, he would have been labeled as a problematic child and not have excelled academically. The bonus was that his self-esteem also went up!

Benji Graves in second grade.

Children should not be put in boxes (meaning labels and expectations) and made to sit still for too many hours. Volunteering in the classroom, I was able to see firsthand that they will learn to make their own decisions, which promotes independent thinking. It was enthralling to see little people move about and know just where to go next. Their happy faces said it all. They were so happy learning!

A standard-based education can be better met through teacher enticement and encouragement. Self-actualized learners absorb challenging curriculum while directing their thinking and mastering challenging information. Enable your students to grow academically as you give them the tools!

READING BECOMES REAL

"The teacher did what?" was the reaction when people heard that we were building a make-believe donut machine. I read to the students daily, even if only for a few minutes, to entice their reading skills and we finished a book that all of the children fell in love with. We had class discussions regarding the characters, writing style, sequence, and plot. Next thing I knew, they were drafting designs and writing about not only making doughnuts but also building a doughnut machine. The entire class collaborated on what a donut machine in days past looked like. Cardboard boxes of every size and dimension arrived and the task began. Our doughnut machine was three-dimensional and stood about six feet high. It took a consensus to assemble the final configuration using bottles of glue and jars of paint. Surveys were taken about favorite kinds of doughnuts and an analysis determined what flavor was best. Recipes were collected, which involved math to triple the chosen recipe and equally assign ingredients to be brought from home. After the doughnuts were consumed and the project went beyond success, students wrote an original play to portray the story to other classes. They also wondered what our next book would be about!

Any book you read with students can come alive in some way. It doesn't have to be this elaborate, but experiences like this even motivate the teacher! If you want to do individual projects or small-group projects instead, think of creative ways to exhibit comprehension: a mobile, poster, sequential chart, or a presentation in which students portray characters. Assign something exciting or give students the choice of how to advertise their book. You'll find reading (or any subject you make exciting) increasing focus and productivity.

Creativity is the special way to stimulate children. Not only does it enhance learning skills, but also I believe that deeper retention is apparent. Besides, why not make learning "fun" as it becomes much more satisfying and enjoyable to the educator, student, and parents?

According to Terri Nelson, a leader in the newspapers throughout Los Angeles:

> So many of today's children find reading boring or difficult and trying to get children to read the books assigned can be very difficult for a parent or teacher. I was very lucky—our teacher made all of the books and stories come alive for us by actually having us recreate parts of stories. I remember one story in particular, *Homer Price and the Donut Machine*. Essentially a woman loses a diamond bracelet while making donuts and rather then having to destroy the whole batch of donuts, Homer comes up with the great idea of selling the donuts and giving a prize to whoever finds the bracelet. As part of the assignment, we actually had a day where we recreated the donut machine and made donuts. One of them had a string in it representing the bracelet and whoever found it won a prize. Every child in that class read the story and was ready for the big day!
>
> By inspiring us this way, Ms. Gail showed us how to involve ourselves in the story to become a part of it and make it real. When this happens, a child wants to read more. I myself am now a voracious reader, churning through thousand-page books weekly. In all, learning to enjoy the process of learning rather then fearing it helps a child to achieve to his or her utmost ability. It is truly what is meant by "growth."

WHAT IS SHE DOING NOW?

I had tweezers and was concentrating on taking the fortunes out of fortune cookies. I was so determined to accomplish this task, but what a project! I could hear their voices in the background, "What is she doing now?"

Individual students, small groups, or an entire class can write fortunes. This type of an assignment generates a lot of thought and discussion. Messages conveyed can be personalized for an individual, family, or occasion. Ask them to make a meaningful and original list. This is a thought-provoking written assignment. Ideas are organized, proofreading is a must, penmanship needs to be legible, and originality is a plus.

Fortune cookies are thoughtful, inexpensive, original creations. Carefully wrapped with cellophane and ribbon, this can be an appropriate gift for any occasion or holiday.

Samples of fortunes the students came up with:

Good health will be with you.

You are very special.	We will have world peace.
Others will listen to you.	You will win a contest.
You will be very happy.	An exciting trip is in your near future.
You will have many friends.	A recent dream will come true.

I confess, the next time I did this, we researched recipes to make our own fortune cookies! We did find it difficult to get the sticky dough to the exact consistency, but when done, our effort was a huge success.

A similar assignment is to make coupon books. Ask students to list ten tasks that would be appreciated by the recipient. Here are some samples of coupons:

This coupon is good for:

I will put my clothes out the night before.	I will fold my own laundry for three loads.
I will stay calm more often.	I will take better phone messages.
I will clean my room and won't complain.	I will try not to be moody.
I will walk the dog daily for four days.	I will be on time for a whole week.

Students can design their book cover as well as the coupons. Students can assemble more than one book for special people in their lives. Personalized coupons for family, neighbor, and babysitter will most likely be redeemed (and maybe even asked for a renewal).

SPECIAL EVENT

The crowd was cheering! The crawdads we had carefully caught in the muddy creek awaited in buckets of water for the race to officially begin. We knew the students' math assignments were finished because the path was carefully measured and clearly marked on the tarp on the floor. Science entries about crustaceans were complete, as were all of the data from our scientific studies.

Students waited in teams as they stood in a large circle surrounding the racetrack. Time clocks were ready and everyone had learned how to use a stopwatch for this important event. And then it began! The competition was close (not so close) and the athletes gave it their best. Some crawdads went forward, others sideways, diagonal, backward, or did not move at all.

News-type articles were written to report the status of each crawdad's skill and feat. Charts were created depicting comparisons of times and distance. The best part of all was hearing the group discussion among the eager contestants that followed: One child said, "It didn't come close to winning, but at least we got to race!" Another said, "We came in fifth but at least ours moved, some of the others weren't even walking."

"Go, go, go, we yelled to the crawdads as slowly each one crept across our racetrack and over the finish line. Some went their own ways, off to the side, or backwards. Mine didn't move at all! We caught them in a creek. We put natural nail polish on them so it didn't hurt them because their shells are hard. This told us their numbers. Science came alive. We guessed, we measured, we graphed and we learned all about our science specimens!" (Shayna, age 10)

"The teacher did what?" my mom said when I called to tell her about my daughter's day at school. Yes, I told her the teacher wanted to excite them about science and she did! I could hear the crowd before I even walked in the door. Gail's cuties surrounded the track and took turns measuring and racing their crawdads. I don't know who was more excited, the kids or the teacher. When the race was over, the children wrote about the activity. The conversation was not about who won, but how lucky they were to participate. I wonder what the teacher will do next?" (Audrey Ludwig, parent)

MAKE IT FUN

In the middle of the anthrax scare, a letter arrived; the return address was from out of state and a name I was unfamiliar with. So, the letter . . . sat there. One morning, as I opened this letter, out fell a picture of a beautiful bride.

Dear Ms. Small,

When you knew me, I was Colleen Kilduff. I moved to California in 1982 and you were my third-grade teacher. I am now twenty-eight, married, and living in Las Vegas, Nevada. One of my relatives who still lives in California saw an article in the paper about you and she wrote to let me know where you are. Just a few weeks ago, I was with these relatives and was telling them about a pa-

Colleen Kilduff in third grade.

per I wrote about you in my college class. I told them I would love to write to you and let you know that you were my reason for becoming a teacher! Ever since third grade, I have wanted to be a teacher and through the years following, when someone would ask me about my school years, I would tell them about you.

I still remember what a great experience your class was and how you made learning so much fun! Everything we learned was exciting and you had a knack for making anything we were learning so much fun. When I was in your class, I was extremely shy and really lacked self-confidence. When I read the article in the paper, one of the things you said was, "Your test scores will go up if you make them feel better about themselves." This was very true in your classroom where you always praised us and made us feel special and important. This is something I hope to do in my future classrooms.

Now I am studying to be a teacher. I know that it can sometimes be a thankless job. Teaching is something you do because you love it and not to make money. So I wanted to let you know that you had an impact in my life and made me want to become a great teacher. I only hope that I can touch someone's life like you touched mine Thank you so much. I am glad that I got the chance to tell you this. I have enclosed a picture of what I looked like then and one of me now. I hope everything is great with you and thank you again!

Sincerely,
Colleen (Kilduff) Soucoup

Bride and collegiate Mrs. Colleen Soucoup.

SCIENCE COMES ALIVE

Don't be afraid to invite people from the outside to address your class about important curriculum. The wealth of information an expert brings is a gift for your students (and could be a lesson for the teacher too).

To quote Chrisy O'Grady,

"The teacher did what?" I could hear parents saying as I carried the baskets and containers back to my jeep. The children were telling their parents about the monitor lizard "Godzilla" who eats venomous scorpions and cobras, the giant tortoise "Tut" who can live over a hundred years, and the albino Burmese python (Hisser) that it took ten kids to hold. Even though my program was over, their excitement and enthusiasm was not. I love visiting schools because children are so eager to learn. What they learn from me doesn't come from a book or the TV.

They get to learn by experiencing! Not only to study up close, but to touch and smell and hold real living animals (specifically reptiles, amphib-

Reptiles visitors (www.reptilefamily.com).

ians, and arthropods—the misunderstood creatures). They are safe for touching and holding because we've raised them with respect. As soon as I let the students know that they would not be forced to touch or hold the animals, a sense of relief spread through the room. It's important for the children to know it is their choice to look, touch or hold. Cool like in "cool!" and cool like in body temperature. Reptiles are cold-blooded. They need an outside source to warm up. Humans are warm-blooded; we make our heat from inside us. We all went on a Safari together and no one even left the classroom. (O'Grady 2001)

If you make your class different from others, your students will not only learn but also vividly remember. Returning students over the years recall specific lessons and concepts, especially the most difficult ones. When learning includes interesting discussions and hands on activities, it becomes far more than pencil and paper.

"The fun things in school were when you made things come alive. Seeing everything we learned in person made learning more fun. Puppet shows, field trips, the park, anything we could see and experience. It is boring to just read about things in a book, but to see them in person and know about them made learning more meaningful and brought books to life. I also liked that everything was hands-on. (Nothing we did was conventional.) All the projects: guessing how many things were in a jar, building a castle from boxes, and having 'ketchup time.' Every day was exciting and creative, and we weren't stuffed inside a classroom. I think the teacher's energy makes school fun and interesting. If the teacher is excited about what he/she is teaching, that makes me interested. I want to know why he/she is so excited, and that inspires me to learn." (Christine Ho)

Gabbie Perret, now a university psychology student, recalls being stimulated by moving to different areas to complete academic tasks. "I remember learning math concepts by counting and comparing all kinds of different things in bins. While learning to read, first we read a book and then it was exciting to make something corresponding to the story. The best part was seeing our projects hung around the room, or on the ceiling, and displayed everywhere. 'Alternate' activities seemed more like 'play' and empowered the learners with not only skills but lifelong knowledge."

⑫

GET OUT OF THE READING BOOKS

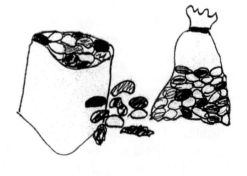

In the everyday curriculum, children don't learn one specific skill to think and solve problems as an individual. There is a strong need to teach students the thinking process that carries throughout their entire education and lifetime. At an early age, students can develop a basis for listening, speaking, and participating. Academic messages can be brought out of students through variant methods. As learning experiences expand, we can open young children's eyes to learn, see, think, and do!

RING TOSS

I was trying to think of a clever way to orally review and reinforce math skills. My criterion was to make something unusual that could be used in or out of the classroom. Learning should be fun and I reflected on carnivals—the games, laughter, and enjoyment. I tried tiddlywinks, flipping discs onto a board or mat with designated numerical values. Even better, get a piece of wood and set it up with sturdy legs. Paint the wood board to make it colorful and enticing. On it put numbers for mathematical facts. Cut holes so that beanbags can be tossed and math will become more fun than imaginable. (Not to mention nonstop—they can't wait to play.) You can put any numbers you want on the board so when the beanbag glides through the hole, math numbers are quickly added, subtracted, multiplied, or divided. This game doesn't have tangible "prizes," it has the discovery of putting numbers together and the feeling of accomplishment. It is the action combined with peer interaction.

OLYMPICS

To share the excitement of an Olympic year is exciting for most of us. (You can always study about the Olympics, even when they aren't happening.) Students of all ages can be involved in related multitask activities. The Olympic games are a world event.

Have students select a country and do research about the flag, team, language, and numerous characteristics. This can be done individually or in collective groups. Have them make colorful posters about their Olympic team, which will not only make a classroom come alive but also enlighten viewers about differences around the world. Students can dress in their team colors, prepare a traditional international food, or share written material about their country.

During an Olympic year, purchase several magazines about the events and athletes that are stimulating/varied reading. Assist students in listing the numerous Olympic events. Alphabetize them or arrange them into categories. Use Olympic words and names of participating countries for vocabulary study, spelling words, or to make a word find. The history of the Olympics and the history of each participating country are educational moments. Comparison math can incorporate where the countries are located: include the distance in mileage and time differences from your school or town. What about the different currencies and the conversion rate? Do your students know the metric system?

Help students to record statistics daily to keep a running tally of Olympic medals earned. Incorporate a class discussion so students understand the honor of the world's best athletes participating in the Olympic games.

Play a tape of beginning and ending Olympic ceremonies for students to hear the music while visually seeing and feeling the impact of the Olympic spirit. Encourage this to extend into the family because the Olympics are watched at home and can be shared and reinforced there also. Assign stories to be written or illustrated about how athletes might feel before, during, and after the competition. Give students a choice of questions to respond to: What is it like to be an Olympian? How does it feel to live in an Olympic village among many nations of the world? Who are Olympians from the United States? Your hometown? What do the Olympic rings represent?

If you have some plain paper (even scratch paper) and markers, you are ready to enjoy a lesson that students will keep asking to do over and over again. First, select judges to score your Olympic participants; then choose students to pretend to do Olympic feats: jumping, dancing, throwing, singing, it doesn't matter at all. Be sure to establish an understanding that this is a fun learning activity; there are no winners and no losers. Eventually, everyone will get to try the different roles.

The Olympic events take place before your very eyes! The judges hold up the official Olympic scores. As the scorecards all go up, students begin to understand the responsibility of being a judge; making decisions of what number (one through ten) best portrays the competitor's performances. Have young students chart and record the different scores and attempt to declare the "winner." Older students can have their first try at averaging multiple numbers. Try making original medals for all to earn and have a class ceremony with students taking turns standing on the pedestals. We have gotten silly with our "competition" and scoring, but the addition of numbers, comparison of numbers, and averaging have become quite proficient.

You might also try scheduling Olympics for physical education to include individual, team, or class events. This has been most successful for end-of-the-year schoolwide activities to add extra spirit and excitement to the last weeks of school.

REAL-LIFE MATH

They can't wait to challenge peers and read their own questions to the class. This is something great to use when you have a few extra minutes and need a filler. The best part of all is having a lesson created by the students themselves!

Writing math word problems demonstrates the understanding of concepts that you have taught. Real-life math can be done in class or as a creative homework assignment. In your directions, tell students you are looking for clarity, logical sequence, explanation of specific mathematical procedure, and reasoning. (Put the answers on the back, hidden under a Post-it note so no one can see the answer!) This helps the presenter to feel secure, just in case a little help is needed. This can be a great review if you are currently studying or finishing a particular type of problem, fact, or math procedure, such as addition, subtraction, multiplication, division, or fractions.

I check student work for accuracy and then keep it in a clip ready for a moment of a quick lesson reinforcement and stimulation. Randomly pull out a student's work and ask them to take it from there. With pride, a student will read their question and try to stump the audience. The answer is "walked" through when a student demonstrates on the board for all to see and review the process of acquiring the correct answer. Examples of some student work:

"I invited ninety-five people to my party. Fifty-four people came and left. How many were still there?"

"If someone came to a party at 3:30 P.M. and the party lasted for two hours and fourteen minutes, what time was the party over?"

"Susie brought home eight cookies and had to share them with her family of four people. How many did each get if they all got the same number?"

"I caught twenty fish. The next day I caught twice as many. How many fish did I catch in all?" Now, if I caught twice as many fish the next time I went fishing, how many would that be? And, if four died, and sixteen fish got away, how many fish did I successfully catch?"

"I went horseback riding with twelve of my friends. Three were tired and stopped on the trail. Two got sick. How many of us finished riding?"

"Mom and dad were married and had four children. They got divorced and dad married someone with three children while mom married someone with two children. How many children in all in this extended family? If each of these children grew up and got married, had three children each, and then divorced, how many children are there now? If they all remarried to someone with twice as many children as they had, what would the total number of children be?"

"My mom and dad ordered two extra-large pizzas. One was pepperoni and one was cheese. In each box there were nineteen slices. The cheese pizza was burned so we had to order another one. How many good pieces of pizza did we finally have in all?"

I always add my true story: my family ordered one large pizza for the Smalls. They delivered a small pizza to the Large family!

NEWS

Many newspapers donate a class set for reading experiences. Looking for a different type of reading lesson? Why not read the newspaper once a week? Reading the newspaper involves numerous overlapping skills that can be fascinating. Working in small cluster groups is a team experience to search for the answers. Once a family, would you believe, asked that I "White-Out" any articles not for children's eyes. So, if you limit the time, they will be so busy finding answers it will alleviate reading any "inappropriate" articles. Make up specific comprehension questions for students to find:

Where is the hottest place in the world today? Where is this country near? What ocean is it near? Name a sports figure and tell why he is being recognized in a newspaper article. How many sections are in the newspaper? How many pages are in each section? If I gave you $10, pick an ad and tell me what you would buy. $100? $3,000? How many styles of print can you find? (Cut and paste a sample of each.) Create a math story problem from data found in the ads. Do a comparison study of which market has the best price for potatoes. Milk? Chicken? Cut out a cartoon, paste it on a paper, and extend the story to give it a different ending. Cut out ten words, paste them on a paper to create a sentence, and use this for a topic sentence to start an original story. What is on television at 3 p.m.? Name four shows that are on at 11 a.m. (The *TV Guide* section is similar to reading an index, a skill most students can use help on.) What are the different times a specific movie is playing? At how many theaters?

TAKING CURRICULUM ONE STEP FURTHER

My students wrote original scripts and songs relating to our many different history units. They were so enthusiastic and filled with energy from viewing historical movies and interviewing people about historical facts. As a result, their research, vocabulary development, and presentation of authentic facts were most interesting and extended the curriculum beyond into a dramatic production. The impression to the audience was amazing at the visual sight of students in colorful outfits as they appeared on stage—"matching" shirts and socks, yet each one of different colors and design.

Are you obligated to do a holiday or special show? Are costumes a necessity and you don't have time nor know what to do? Ask the children to bring a plain white t-shirt and a pair of white socks too. (If that isn't possible, buy some in bulk and maybe try a fundraiser for the expense.) Study color wheels and the components of color. Read about art techniques through the ages. In science, study resistance, which is the technique of batik and tie-dye. Children often don't tie the string secure enough for effective resistance, so double rubber band the areas for the best result. Place rubber bands around each sock to get a stripe design (or on each sleeve). Separate the front and back of the tee shirt so that each will have an artistic effect. Using gloves, dip the shirts and socks into different colors of permanent dye. Try the same process with torn sheets or scrap material (even paper towels), and you can hang them in the classroom to add a touch of artistic colorful décor to the room environment. Let everything dry thoroughly so that when you do pull off the rubber bands you will all marvel at the magic and mystery of resistance. Your creations are perfect to wear on field trips or for a special activity. (This project can be done with your class or even an entire grade level.) The best part is that they stand out yet each one is a totally individual creation. Just like the students.

GO WITH THE MUSIC

The karaoke machine is a tool that I never imagined could enhance a student's reading skills, self-confidence, and eagerness to learn. Sarah was new to my class. Her reading level was low as was her self-esteem. She was shy and withdrawn, often in her own world. She rarely talked but she watched. One day, a child brought in a karaoke machine for her oral report. She did a presentation that incorporated music and words. As the music began, the students came alive and involved. I saw Sarah look, heard her hum, and before I knew it she was not only participating but had the microphone in her hand. She was loudly singing the words as she watched them on the screen. So here we have a method to get fluency in a user-friendly way! I also found the karaoke machine useful in generating writing, application of formulas and concepts, and an effective means of student retention. I recommend karaoke as an activity for a school/community "Reading Night" to increase fluency and promote the desire to read.

THE GREAT DEBATE

Give students a topic and let them go! Depending on the topics of choice, students can read, research, watch appropriate videos, or interview adults with knowledge pertaining to a topic. I remember giving an assignment "Read about it! It's your country! Find out why it is so special!" The debate was a hot one about events leading up to the Declaration of Independence. (Who was involved? Why people did what? What about the colonists? King? Englishmen? War? Taxes? Common Sense?)

I've found with debates that students will identify their personal thoughts on an assigned topic and work in peer groups to find a way to prove their point. Once they are motivated, there is no stopping them. Establish a time for the debate, select an adult to mediate, invite an audience, and you will be amazed at the foundation and knowledge the students somehow come up with. (And it's all right out of the books; it is them, sharing and deciphering newfound knowledge.)

In every social science curriculum, there is a component for students to recognize how ideas, individuals, and events have developed our history.

Early grades also involve children in understanding the people who supply our daily needs and the interdependence of crops, food, and workers in the process. Students should be made aware of people who make a difference in their lives now as well as in the past. Brainstorm names of famous people. Include library time to introduce biographical books as well as fiction and nonfiction. Extend student thinking by helping them prepare meaningful questions to learn about past history and important events. Students can pretend to be a reporter and interview people about history, contrasts, and development over the years. History is made up of people, so examining real human experiences can have lasting impact (or they can create an "interview" from facts read about in books). Other possibilities include mapping, charting, and graphing information. A timeline is a valuable account and a visual portrayal of history and events. A class chart will collectively display timely changes in clothing, transportation, communication, and traditions. Books, maps, and media are all available—yet far more impressionable is a student who can personally connect and respond to history.

You can find seniors in your community who would thrive by being able to share with students of today's generation. Together, you can adapt an appealing history lesson that will maintain interest and stimulate learning. Students can write human-interest stories using factual messages that might also be highlighted through illustrations.

I teach my students wherever we go that everything is a part of the learning process. When we bring our experiences together, we enrich our curriculum. Ruthie came into my life a few years ago and I realized the opportunities we have today through her enduring tales. When I shared my story with my class about my friend Ruthie as she turned 100, spontaneously written notes were sent to her. History became reality the day Ruthie came to school. Her vivid stories and pictures of the land and orange groves where Disneyland now stands engaged my students. Ruthie's historical recount beautifully segued into our integrated thematic studies. She gave my students the gift of wisdom. In turn, they gave to her a giant heart of candy kisses that they had made. On it, they put their ages, which all together added up to 158!

When learning stems from excitement and pleasure, it is not forgotten. When you bring in visitors who make your lessons become real, a lasting impression is left on your students. They took risks, writing original songs to express themselves through rhythm and music because we had learned to play our washboards, thimbles, and spoons. I told Ruthie the children would write about life now and then and about our special day together with her. When Ruthie left, children wrote about what they had learned:

"It was hard to get around because they had to ride in a stagecoach. Kids didn't have things we have today because they didn't even have electricity. It was hard just to get milk because you had to milk the cows first. In Ruthie's days they got a lot of disease. I am glad Ruthie is so healthy and she will be 101."

"They had to cut down trees to build their houses. They hunted for their food and life was not so easy then. They did not make cars like us and they often used horses to get around. They made the things that they had and they would watch the sun set."

"She said she lived on a farm when little. She never got in much trouble when she was in school. She had red hair when she was little and young. She looks like she is 70 years old, but really she is 100! She is so pretty. She said no one knew and not to tell, but she wrote stories for her sisters because she had an imagination and they did not. They only took baths once a week back then."

"I wonder how it looked a hundred years ago? I was not born that day so now I am learning. I wonder if it was scary? They had to walk miles to school in those days."

"You couldn't just go to the store for things so they had to make them. They didn't have games to play like we do. I think they had to get along more with each other. I wouldn't have wanted to wear a dunce cap or sit in the corner!"

"They didn't have refrigerators then. Stoves were made out of wood and things because they didn't have anything else. It was hard to wash their clothes. Ruthie's brother got hit in the face by a cow's tail. Ruthie ate a cookie that we made, then she left with all the things that we made for her and a smile."

"One hundred years ago they had to bake their own cookies because you couldn't buy them. They had all-grade schools. You got whipped if you answered a question wrong in school. They didn't have television and they made their wine by hand. There were wagon trains, horses, and buggies. When cars first began they were called horseless carriages and it was hard to get around back then."

"One dollar was worth a lot more than a dollar today. I wonder what they dreamed about a hundred years ago?"

The children's stories describing history via Ruthie were shared throughout the school and community. To our surprise, Ruthie wrote too. A letter arrived in the mail, which students read and reread with such pleasure and excitement:

Dear Gail,

You have made me do more thinking, which is good for me, and how it feels to be 100. How wonderful it was to be met by kids carrying a large banner to welcome me. I think of my trip out to your school and the won-derful children. They must be a joy to their parents. It is easy to see that learning does not come from books, but comes from living.

My school was a one-room schoolhouse. To get there, my sister, brothers and I walked 1-1/4 mile each day, except when it snowed and my dad took us in a bobsled. When I was young, we didn't go to the bak-ery to buy bread or rolls. My mother made them all. So the joy my brothers, sister, and I had after school was coming home when my mother had baked bread. She always included a pan of biscuits too. We would break them open and spread them with freshly churned butter. After that, we would change to work clothes, and go to work with farm chores. There were always things to do, such as working in the garden and hoeing to keep the ground loose. This is just a sample of my life then. Women worked very hard, with very few conveniences, but were happy doing it.

In my time, electricity was not installed. Your questions were thinking ones about life without electricity. How did we keep food cold? The food was lowered into the wells for water, which was very deep and cold. So when food was needed, it was pulled back up out of the well. Our laundry was done with a tub of water and a washboard. It was quite a job to get it cleaned and rinsed well. It was hung on a line to dry. We didn't have an electric iron, it was a solid, heavy iron heated on a stove.

The cows were brought in from pasture twice a day, and were milked by hand. Kids had to learn how to milk and how to sit on a milk stool. Those cows were not always real happy and sometimes kicked the bucket over.

Learning comes from living. My day was very enjoyable. It brought back old times and made me think more. I took with me your 100 candy kisses and where the children had written their names and ages, which added up to 158. The children asked me what it was like to be 100 all in one person. From the interest your children showed during my visit, I could tell they are anxious to learn.

Love to all, Ruthie.

13

ORAL REPORTS

One year, as I was locking the door for the summer, a little girl came running up to me. I could see she had something very important in her hand as she ran towards me waving it. "If I'm in your class next year, I know what I want to do for my oral report," she whispered while also out of breath. On the paper in her hand was her childlike writing, "I will make a rainbow." What a great idea, I told her! Rainbows actually are one of my favorite things because I love the colors, brilliance, and wonder. She was in my class the next year, and gave a presentation on colors and prisms. This child confirmed for me that children can look forward to working independently and exploring a choice of an oral report project.

Charlene

If you can bring your joys and passions into your classroom, your students will be encouraged to find and express theirs. When you can share something with your children every day, you are establishing a rapport as you give them "an oral report" on an ongoing basis. Students value your experiences and tales, and begin to develop and express their own original thoughts. When you create an environment encouraging children as individuals to "shine," they are more apt to participate and become truly involved in their education.

I set the tone for oral reports at the beginning of the school year and students are juiced by my enthusiasm. I tell them that there will be a day when they can teach the class. This becomes a way of life. Knowing their choices are wide open, they often look for a way to entertain and educate their peers. When an oral report project is explained to the students with a positive attitude, the question merely becomes: When do I present it? I place a sign-up calendar on the wall and watch it fill with children's names and original ideas.

Children actually "teach the class" and better understand what it is that teachers do every day. They appreciate the effort that goes into planning and preparing each lesson. As long as children think it through, there are no limits as they delve into their projects. Students seek their own interests. Maybe there is something that they have always wanted to know or discover. This is their opportunity to choose, initiate, create, and investigate a topic of interest. The use of common household items in these projects is fascinating as students rise to meet the challenge.

The actual presentations take from ten minutes to a half-hour. Then, I tell them to "take it on the road." I encourage them to go to other teachers in the school, regardless of grade level, and ask if they can give their presentation to reach other children. This becomes a cross-age experience. This empowers the presenter and opens new possibilities for the listeners.

Have students keep a log of the oral reports in which notes, a written response, or an illustration are included. They can record what they have learned, new vocabulary, or even how to do the project at home. After a presentation, a group discussion is a valuable communication tool. It is in these group follow-up sessions that positive qualities about a project are contributed. This builds self-esteem for the presenter as classmates share that they have listened and learned. Students look forward to this process because it is satisfying and fulfilling.

If necessary, you might give students ideas for their oral reports. It is important to allow the student to make the actual choice. I prefer an open-ended project and am often amazed at what students come up with. Once, though, a child wasn't prepared and wasn't satisfied with the results. She wrote me a letter about how much she learned from not being prepared. She asked for another chance. Her second report was a well thought-out effective project. This was a true educational experience for all of us because it elicited many meaningful discussions.

I recommend doing oral reports the last month of school because they become a special experience for everyone. This is usually a time when books are getting turned in, lessons are winding down, and "summeritis" has set in not only for students but often for teachers too. It is a way to keep focus and interest alive even to the last day of school.

I have been told that many people feel speaking in front of an audience is one of the most fearful experiences one can encounter. Incorporating choices, motivation, respect, circle, and self-esteem into a solid curriculum allows students to take risks and is a great confidence builder. Students learn how to "stand on their own two feet" and look for chances to "glow." Some students even "dress up" and assume a character or special identity. Like anything, if you tell them they can do it, they will!

As an educator, it is fulfilling watching the progress of the students as they evolve to become who they are in the final days of the school year. When a child gets up to give his or her oral report, it gives me tears because they are standing on their own two feet. They've made a choice, they've cultivated a passion, and are openly sharing themselves with others. It's amazing to me to think that some of these kids started the year as quiet, shy, and dependent children.

I would like to share some comments of elementary children about oral reports:

"It feels good to teach the class. That's what oral reports are all about. How many kids get to teach their own class? Some people get nervous and I don't think they should. If friends are prepared, it will go smoothly and the time goes fast. Before you know it, everyone is telling you how great you did. When I get to present to another class, I feel important and happy. I meet new people I never knew before and when I see them again, they are newfound friends that smile and know a little bit about me." (Micaela)

"I felt good because I was doing a different thing that I had never done before. I took notes first and planned my project. I even made a model to show the class. I practiced so that this would be a positive experience. I was scared until it felt good that I was sharing and helping everyone enjoy my oral report. I taught them how to make puppets. No two puppets came out the same! The puppets suddenly seemed almost real and each had a personality all its own." (Jade)

"My uncles and aunts thought it was crazy that I had to do an oral report. You know what? It wasn't crazy and I have to tell you that it was fun. I got to teach myself, my teacher, and classmates. It took a while to think about all of this and then suddenly da daa . . . the topic came to me. I wasn't afraid because I practiced on my brother, sister, parents, and friends. Some people I know practiced on their dogs, or in front of the mirror on the wall. I couldn't wait to get it over with and then I didn't want it to end." (Conner)

Kendra "Do you really have to do an oral report?"

"I felt proud of myself because I attempted something I had never done before and it worked! Plus, it taught me (and my teacher) something new! I had an adult help me because a match had to be lit to make an egg go through a bottle with a small mouth. And it really did!" (Adrian)

"Once I heard someone ask, "Do you really have to do an oral report?" I am always thrilled to have the opportunity to teach the class. A new topic is always what I pick. Delightful hands-on things are what I choose. Last year, I did ice cream volcanoes, and now I am preparing on the subject of miniscule Japanese gardens. For some people, you would have to be fearless to get up in front of a class and give an oral report. For me and others, it would only be a daily habit. You see, I feel good about me and I know that I will do the best I can do!

Oral reports take lots of research, though—but all that research really pays off! You get a successful oral report. These are the things that you need: determination, research, brains, supplies, confidence, and curiosity. And, you know, all of these can be found. Oral reports help you in life by teaching you how to deal with the questions, pursue new knowledge, and by helping you to organize yourself. This experience increases self-confidence and will help you throughout your whole life." (Kendra)

Yes, in first grade, this same talented Kendra did an oral report entitled "Famous Volcanoes." She used exact diagrams and did a factual comparison of Mount Vesuvius and the Hawaiian islands. Upon completion of quoting her extensive research data and references, we shared a tasty, hands-on creative volcanic experience. I will share the original project with you in hopes that you will truly visualize the excitement and participation that transpired: "Huge mounds of ice cream represent the volcanoes, which are surrounded by lava rocks and boulders, as well as green vegetation. Molten strawberry sauce flows freely from the cauldron, which is clearly identified by the characteristic maraschino cherry at its peak. Sometimes giant rings of whipped cream smoke and clouds are seen encircling the peak.

Hailey Hersh:
how to scramble eggs.

Oral reports build enthusiasm and personal greatness for the children. I want to include ideas from some projects that have been done over the years. Please appreciate the variety and include a smile when you imagine what some of these were really like: How to Make Whipped Cream, How to Train Your Cat (including a shy cat for the demo), How to Make a Paper Cup (and fill it with water!), Sign Language, Making Quicksand, Peanut Butter Playdough, Making a Volcano (assistance to make them erupt), Soda Bottle Animals, Felt/Yarn Animals, Scrambled Eggs (breaking the shell and cooking them), Tie-Dye, Mirror Images–Symmetry, Squishy Matter, Languages (varied reports teaching Spanish, Hebrew, or Japanese), Masks, God's Eyes, How to Make a Rocket, Collages, Taking/Comparing Fingerprints, How a Chemical Reaction Inflates a Balloon, Sculptures, Electromagnets, Weaving, Pinwheels, Making a Calendar (as in which months have how many days?), How to Make a Sundae (similar to taco, ice cream nachos, no bake cookies, smoothies, and more), Color Wheels, Terrariums, Making Paper, Rock Houses (Rock People), Pennants, Piñatas, Squishing Oranges into Juice, Balloon Animals, Friendship Bracelets, Writing a Newspaper, Making an Original Hat, Becoming a Clown, and the list goes on.

A favorite was a simple project about peas (different kinds of peas—in the pod, canned, frozen, and a thorough explanation about all; we even went outside to actually plant peas). I also enjoyed a "blind tasting" in which different beverages were tasted and rated. "Will the students be able to guess the name of drink #1 and drink #2? I'm hoping to discover a few facts in doing this test." (I actually blindfolded the good-natured presenter afterwards to see if he could tell the difference, and he could.)

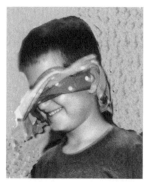

Conner Jadwin: blind tasting.

A student who was just mastering English at the time did a significant oral report. She had drawn a map of Guatemala and explained her heritage to her classmates. She directed how to draw the map, including a key showing oceans, and surrounding topography. Open discussion included different dialects within a country as well as varied traditional tamale recipes from different areas. Her long hair was intricately braided with colorful ribbons and her smile told more than words. Another exceptional report was by a young girl wanting to be an architect "when she grew up." A chart depicted a plan as she explained the intricate details of design and architecture. Classmates were asked to plan something in writing and to carry out their design building with the sugar cubes she then gave to them. Afterward, students wrote in detail about sugar cube buildings and the actual application using mathematical data for their projection. (Although a third grader designed this lesson, it could be expanded into an entire study or unit at any level.)

My all-time favorite was a darling little six-year-old girl who came dressed up in a white fluffy dress as the Tooth Fairy, complete with her wand. Our paths just crossed again; Suzie Hoctor is now studying at the university and majoring in journalism:

I strongly believe starting public speaking at a young age can mold a person forever. I remember when I lost my two front teeth and my mom decided to dress me up in my white communion dress to turn me into the toothless tooth fairy. So my experiences in public speaking began and I fearlessly enjoyed it. I know many people have a fear of public speaking, but for me it came naturally. Since I started at such a young age, the words "I can't" never occurred to me. I believe you can accomplish anything in life, once you set your mind to it.

Through oral reports, students think, interpret, understand, and communicate. Listeners are taught to value individual interests and treat each other with respect. The students use experience, curiosity, and  imagination to create a subject significant to them. In reality, an "oral report" doesn't have to be limited to a school assignment. It could be done as a home activity to encourage a family to explore something together on a "nothing to do" day.

ORAL REPORT FACT SHEET

Choose a topic that is exciting and interesting to you. Be original, organized, prepared, and thorough in your presentation. Have fun while learning. I can't wait to see you share your newfound knowledge.

Written report: explaining your topic (20 points)—Include your rough draft as an indication of your process, editing, and progress in achieving your oral report.

Visual material: precut and ready to go, including a sample (20 points)—To help your presentation go smoothly, make a poster showing the step-by-step process to help your audience better understand your project.

Interesting: captivating (20 points)

Good speaking voice: loud and clear (10 points)

Clean up after presentation (10 points)

Available and able to answer questions (10 points)

Other (10 points)

MISTEAKS

Presentation of any instructional material takes on meaningful direction when interesting diversions are applied. Students conscious that mistakes take them new places acquire momentum and are not discouraged easily. Growth from mistakes is an essential ingredient in growing up.

It is okay to make a mistake! We learn from mistakes and usually that lesson, no matter how big or how small, is one that is long remembered. A mistake enables us to learn and move forward with newly found knowledge. Recognizing this, children might take that extra step to discover new things that they might have been afraid to try.

One of the things I tell parents is to let their children know when they themselves make a mistake. The same is true for teachers at all levels. How exciting it is when a young child (anyone) finds that someone else makes mistakes too. I once heard that even chocolate chip cookies were a mistake that somehow got discovered! Somewhere it must be written that pencils have erasers for a reason?

While in Japan as an ambassador, I was honored at a special luncheon that was like a royal banquet. The food was artistically prepared and presented. Each flavor and bite was better than the last. The service was on fine china with gold trim on a linen tablecloth. My waiter bowed and set down a bowl of their specialty, sweet potato soup. It tilted and spilled onto the crisp white linen. The commotion that ensued was astounding. Not only the quick, overdone clean up, but also the bowing, apologies, and disgrace. The soup had not spilled on my clothes and it was only soup in the first place.

Suddenly, the whole restaurant was involved in one little spill. I wished I could have done something for the poor waiter who now appeared so pale in the face. In front of everyone, he was admonished and removed by his supervisor. At the completion of this luncheon, I would not leave until the supervisor brought the waiter back for me to see.

When I travel, I always have little presents with me (just in case) and I gave a present to the waiter. I also gave one to that manager who had become (I thought) so overly concerned over the whole incident. I explained to him (through the help of interpreters) that it is okay to make mistakes. These are only little things that don't make such a difference in a lifetime.

When my driver was about to leave, I looked out of the window and there at curbside were the waiter and the supervisor waving good-bye with huge grins from ear to ear. I leaned out of the window and we all smiled and waved to each other. I sat back and thought maybe I had reached out and made a difference. I looked back once again and I could see as we drove away, they both had pinned onto their uniform the little gold California pins that I had given them. That, actually, was a highlight of my trip. (Something I must remember to tell my students!) Someone (adults) had just learned that it is okay to make a mistake!

It is important for children to recognize that everyone makes mistakes. We all make them, but recognizing them, having them called to our attention, is so important. The fear of being wrong, the fear of making a mistake, keeps students from venturing out. People equate mistakes with "failure." They can learn that there are rewards in mistakes.

We learn from errors, even minor ones. Sometimes when it is called to our attention, we may not have even realized the mistake. After corrections are made or acknowledged, then life goes on. Often children stumble because they do not understand something. When you instill in them that mistakes are natural and a growing process, and when they truly believe it, then they will be more comfortable and eager to try. As the teacher, it is how you handle student errors and incorrect responses that says it all. There is no "wrong answer" if your response is appropriate. Use these as excellent learning tools to strengthen misunderstanding, curiosity, and competence.

Children have a need (and the right) to feel "safe" every day in their school setting. Help them not to "worry" as you teach them to adapt and to go forward with each learning experience. Some children are afraid (embarrassed?) to give a wrong answer, and they tune you out or are unable to take the necessary risks in school (in life?). Persistence is when people believe in themselves knowing that they are doing their best. As an educator, nurturing students to contribute (right or wrong) has an effect on everything you teach. Encourage children to voice their opinions and develop the sensitivity of classmates to listen. Foster the acceptance of a genuine wrong answer and empower students to learn from each other as well as to grow from every opportunity

My philosophy is that a comfortable student in a positive learning environment will "step up to the plate" and give his best. Sometimes children are unsuccessful at something and just give up. Teaching determination is important so they can discover why and pursue to find answers. They need to learn from the mistakes because they tell us the direction we need to go or practice. Mistakes are necessary on the road to discovery. How many times is a child unintelligible while learning to talk? Is it a mistake that a baby falls down many times while learning to walk?

An "accident" often leads to inventions and new knowledge. Christopher Columbus "discovered" America and is an example of a mistake that involves us! If you tell children it takes intelligence to overcome a mistake, they will show you they are smart enough to learn from it. Who knows? If you explain the concept of patents and trademarks, a struggling student now may be the genius of invention in the future!

Every morning there is a language lesson on the board for children to read and copy correctly. These sentences are purposely written incorrectly.

(I can't tell you how many times I have written one correctly by mistake!) I try to create sentences that are interesting, sometimes amusing, or about topics of current interest.

Sometimes I write a paragraph that contains mistakes. Children rewrite what I have written using correct grammatical form. This includes spelling, vocabulary, punctuation, and sentence structure. Often you might hear a giggle when a student recognizes the numerous errors, indicating true learning as the necessary corrections are made. I find class time each day to review these mistakes while all students watch, listen, and participate. Because of this oral interpretation, valuable concrete language skills are recognized and reinforced. As time goes on, students become more skilled and aware to begin self-editing their written work. Some students tell me that correcting sentences that seemed irreparable best teaches them the criteria for proper language structure.

The same format is used daily in my math classes. Students come back years later and tell me of the importance of this process. They acknowledge essential skills they came to understand (and master) because of correcting mathematical errors. Specifically, by listening and recognizing corrections while applying rules and using reasoning, students absorb and transfer knowledge. I find the secret is the exposure of every learning situation possible and instilling in students that they can do it.

I always remember what I once heard, "It's not a mistake unless you refuse to correct it."

Helping students to recognize and learn from mistakes can also be done through collaborative writing experiences. A cooperative group reading and sharing the rough draft of an originally written story brings attention to elaboration and worthwhile remodeling. Through the reconstruction process, mutual creativity ensues to enhance the triumphant final project.

Jessica explains, "I used to write one sentence or maybe two. One day I discovered I could do more, so I began writing about animals. My whole family didn't understand why I was edited so we all had to have a conference with an interpreter. We learned I was not in trouble, I was challenged and becoming who I am today!"

I am never late. But I was! I ran into my class a few minutes after the lunch bell. What I saw was something I will never forget—my students were sitting in our daily circle and had started . . . without me! The significance of that moment exemplified every educator's goal—for students to apply the skills you instill in them and to be independent.

Cathy, a child who a few years ago struggled with language and relationships, had taken on the leadership. With her newly found confidence and composure, she mimicked my every word and I stayed back to watch her/them continue: "Thank you." "I am glad everyone is listening." "What do you think about that?" "That is unique." "We understand." With a smile, she encouraged her peers to participate and interact.

A remarkable class discussion followed about my "mistake" and what we learned from it. I contacted her family to include them on this accomplishment. Because of this day, every Thursday (it happened on a Thursday) students take turns having the opportunity to assume the leadership role. Subsequently, they are now more aware of the components that make our circle successful and meaningful.

Dr. Brenda Yoshinaga, a parent volunteer, has entertained my students over the years with her amazing scientific presentations. She tells colorful stories, even one about mistakes in laboratories, and about the implications of success as a result of trial and error in science. The scientific process and mathematical discoveries my students participate in inspire them in all areas of academics. Dr. Yoshinaga stressed to the children the value of mistakes that sometimes can affect the entire world. With watchful eyes, she used descriptive diagrams, and explained that penicillin was discovered only by mistake. She described bacteria, platelets, mold, culture, and the accidental discovery of penicillin by Alexander Fleming. Besides all that, she noted that the mistake also won the honor of a Nobel Prize.

Cooking, as well as science, is a multisubject approach that merits discovery and learning. The research, discussion, planning, and gathering of ingredients is in itself a lesson in preparation and responsibility. The measuring (equivalents/fractions) is hands-on learning, adding another dimension to required math skills. Kids will be kids! No matter how well planned an exciting cooking lesson appears, someone almost always forgets, misplaces, or drops an ingredient. As with all lessons, a teacher must be able to modify and redirect. We have improvised and reconfigured recipes to overcome what seems an irreconcilable mistake into an

original rendition. Thus, new recipes (concoctions) have been celebrated by students who have renamed the original recipe "The Mistake." Everything we have ever cooked at school has been eagerly consumed by the "cooks" and that is the true testimony to mistakes!

When I make a mistake, the students feel challenged to tell me.
Whether it is writing the wrong date on the board or an error in a note
to go home. (And we all make mistakes!) Better to have something cor-
rected than to overlook it or just forget it. Think of how they feel when
they get it right!

You know, there are many kinds of chocolate chip cookies. Somehow,
you might just discover the best one by mistake! It is almost a game and
I encourage parents to also reveal their mistakes, no matter how insignificant. Parents don't "lose" if they claim their errors. They share
honesty and gain more respect with their kids. Mistakes are meaningful
because a foundation begins for a child to better accept his or her mistakes while building better self-esteem and character at the same time.

One day, a natural flow existed in my working classroom as all students were engrossed in a serious and challenging learning activity. Two
students, astutely aware, came up to me smiling to fully inform me that
they observed my secret and mistake. (Funny, I didn't know!) They assumed that because I had on two different black shoes that I was testing them to acknowledge such an overt mistake. This instructional moment created a lot of attention and was better than one I could have
possibly planned. I told the truth, that I had no idea I was wearing two
different shoes, and was not even embarrassed because my students all
know that it is okay to make mistakes. Together, we shared a good laugh
and a valuable moment in teaching!

THOSE THINGS EVERYONE IS ALWAYS TALKING ABOUT

Every school district has its own criteria, process, and grading format. Grading is a means of accountability in education, yet along with it there also needs to be a way for students to fully understand how they are doing.

Keep a log so that you can easily, regularly, and privately record information and insight on each student. (I have tried notes to myself, files, and also envelopes stashed in the back of the cupboard.) For efficiency and ease, however, set up a book with a tab or section for each child. Keep it in one (confidential) place, so it is easy to jot down a note that might be helpful or pertinent later. Documentation helps when it comes to conferences and written reports because if it's written down, you won't have to rack your brain later. Maybe an extra comment as to how a student did something special! A suggestion that you noted might be of help for a particular child in reaching goals. Place thoughts you want to be sure to remember after a conference, or something a child has shared that you don't want to forget. Is there something you want to remember to share with a child or his or her parent?

CONFERENCES

One-on-One Conferencing

I believe there should be an "appointment" for every child before his or her progress report or report card goes home. At this conference, I suggest meeting in a private corner to fully discuss accomplishments, goals, and ways to improve. It is a means of communication so there are no surprises when the report card goes home. It enhances the teacher-child relationship because the child feels more valuable and this is a special time to talk together without interruption. This process encourages independence because children think and speak for themselves, as together we are addressing individual needs. A child may have a question or sometimes an explanation that might enlighten a teacher as to how to help this individual child.

The Conference

Be sure students understand the purpose of the conference so there is no hesitation or worry. (With very young children, you might first role-play to set the tone about what to expect in your meeting.) Discuss the meaning and value of constructive criticism. Explain how we can all grow from this. It is a difficult concept for anyone, especially a child. Establish a positive feeling so students look forward to extra time with you, the teacher, on a one-to-one basis.

Encourage children to bring with them thoughts, ideas, or questions they want to ask you. (Is there something they really want to know? What about? What if I did? Can I?) If the other students are in the classroom while you are conferencing, be sure they understand the importance of not interrupting unless it is an emergency. Stress the importance of confidentiality. What you and a child discuss is between the two of you and the family (and not all the other children in the class).

I have three positive things written down about students that I give to them at our meeting. It is something tangible for them to see and have.

(Something to start on the bright side!) Usually, these are comments I put on the progress report or report card. This is modeling and builds the confidence too. (Maybe a student has improved in peer relationships, being on time, or has a better attitude.) There is always something positive to share.

Plan specific questions that you are going to ask a child. (On an individual basis, is there something you've really been wanting to discuss?) Identify information, good or bad, that you feel a need to convey. Ask a student to measure his or her work and behavior. Talk to them. They can't or won't make changes unless they see a reason to. Gain insight into student self-awareness.

Take notes for your records and to give to your student. (Individual goals and strategies you reach. Something you can refer to at a future conference.) What information does the student need to process and improve on? Give specific steps or strategies to help implement objectives. Determine if or when a follow-up conference should be scheduled. A conference is a collaborative effort where together you review and evaluate skills, behaviors, student progress, and needs.

The Parent Conference

Actually, I feel the same guidelines can be followed for meaningful parent-teacher conferences. Begin with positive statements or compliments about their child. Make eye contact and express your belief in establishing a mutual collaborative relationship. If you are not in regular contact with parents, you might send a preconference letter home. Describe your conference objectives, what you hope to accomplish, and how you are looking forward to meeting them.

If you establish comfortable, open communication with a family, a conference is like a gold mine. Together with the parents, you can work cooperatively and productively to accomplish far-reaching results. If in the conference you verbalize problems or concerns and suggested remedies, determine the follow-up plan. What do you (and the parents) need to reach solutions? Always encourage discussion to learn about family dynamics as well as students' interests, abilities, and weaknesses. Help parents to discover the best, most efficient direction to encourage and guide their child towards fulfilling experiences.

A TRUE STORY

You never know! Sometimes parents over the years have told me the most amazing things about their children. (You know, those hard-to-believe stories!) This one was in reverse: an "angel" named Joel who could do no wrong. I often thought it was not "normal" for a child to never make a mistake or misbehave. When I told the family that I was worried about their child always being "perfect," they said, "he only acts like that at school." They asked me for suggestions regarding the contrasts of the child's unacceptable behaviors in the home. (I took it as self-defense or denial about the mention of perfectionism.)

A few months later, I was with friends at Magic Mountain in one of the cute, intriguing little gift shops. I heard a lot of noise and confusion nearby. My friends had been outside where the artificial snow was and came running in to get me, saying, "There is a child outside; you would die if you ever had one like that in your class!" They went on excitedly telling me that this child was using profanity, screaming, and throwing snowballs and dirt at everyone within range. The management of the amusement park had been consulted. When I eventually did wander outside, there he was! The "angel" I had lost sleep over because he was so perfect.

Sometimes the best-behaved child at school is the opposite at home. The behaviors discussed and interpreted in a conference can make a difference for everyone! Be nonjudgmental, patient, and listen to what a parent is saying. (Listen first, before you advise.) Little things you might learn about a child might make a world of difference for you, the teacher.

THE REPORT CARD

A report card is an exchange of information about a student's academic progress, work habits, and citizenship. It is a subjective assessment and description of student accomplishments. The written format and the number of semesters (trimesters) vary by district and state. Whatever the form, the intention is an official notification given to parents regarding student growth.

Include a note home with the report cards indicating that it is a documentation of "what a student has earned." Ask parents to especially look for the qualities that show dedication and improvement on the part of the student. If the comment sections are a part of the formal report, indicate both strengths and weaknesses. (Remember, too, there are ways you can word recommendations for improvement.) Examples: Susie needs to make better use of time; Jack needs to be aware of how his behavior affects others, Karen has potential to improve if (fill in the blank), Johnny has qualities for academic success in (subject) but needs assistance in (subject), Margie needs to work on improving (subject). I struggle with "grades" because students are each so individual and competence is the level I want each to attain.

Teacher Report Card

When is the last time you received a report card? How did it make you feel? Were comments included to provide an opportunity for you to recognize strengths or to improve performance? Were there any "surprises?" I believe an effective teacher gains significant insight from a "teacher report card." It can be any form you desire (depending on the level you teach) but gives students a chance to reveal or evaluate their experiences.

First, you will need to set guidelines for your students and include discussion about why a report card is valuable for you too. Next, determine what will be "graded." How do the students feel about homework, school, teacher, classmates, and specific subjects? Why? What would they like added (deleted) in the curriculum? Favorite lesson?

You might use a coloring graph to fill in spaces about selected activities or subjects that indicate likes and dislikes; maybe a point system, one through ten; or possibly a written evaluation regarding specific subject, concepts, or methods. Going into this, know that you can't "please" everyone and not to take your report card too personally. Be aware, however, that through your students' guidance, you might discover something new and valuable.

Parent Report Card

In a group writing assignment with my students, we created a "mock" report for the volunteers who help and support our program. We

rewrote the words, using the actual (approximate) report card form. We
included:

- Comments: Thank you for being you!
- Effort: Excellent/the best!
- Subjects (qualities) of evaluation that we listed and "graded": Supportive, patient, dependable, understanding, helpful, enthusiastic,
  good listener, interested, friendly, smart, creative, productive, inspiring, laughter, caring and . . . well-behaved.
- Improvement needed: Us—telling you how much we appreciate all
  that you do!

Oh, yes, one more thing: These report cards go home in sealed envelopes properly addressed to those so in need!

HOMEWORK

Most students participate in homework assignments based on the expectations of a district, teacher, or class. I think that homework should
be a meaningful reinforcement of academic principles previously introduced by the teacher (and there are times when a teacher should modify the content, process, amount, or product to meet the differentiated
needs of an individual student).

Appropriate homework should be designed to increase practice and
better grasp classroom instruction. Sometimes it moves a child beyond
"facts" to better interpretation and understanding. Instruction should
clearly define how to do an assignment before it goes home. Remind
parents that the best help is not the answers, but thoughtful questions
that guide a child into thinking along the right track.

I used to assign homework for a certain night and expect it to be returned the following day. (Actually, we could each probably write an entire book giving the amazing excuses as to why homework wasn't returned.) Finally, I came to the realization of a method that works better
for me and my students. Every Friday, I give them an assignment sheet
for the next week. I find that this defines what we are doing and where

we are going. Day by day, it spells out any special activities as well as the homework to be completed. It is due the following Friday as they walk in the door. Now, visits from Grandma, soccer practice, ballet lessons, baseball games, and even birthdays no longer "interfere" with homework. It doesn't matter any more when homework is done or in what order because it is each child's responsibility to budget their week and complete their work.

Homework now comes in like clockwork! First, I check to be sure it is turned in and then I check for understanding and accuracy. Encouraging students to have a good attitude about homework enables them to feel their own progress as well as accomplishment. Yes, some basic skills do need repetition and refinement. Ask yourself, though, if you can make an assignment appealing, intriguing, and inviting to your students. Craft an assignment to stretch skills and performance while at the same time encourage students to want to go on a quest to seek the answers. Key principles can demonstrate concrete learning in a multiple of "different" ways!

Here is an example of a Thanksgiving break homework assignment: Talk to a family member, grandma, grandpa, aunt, uncle, or member of the extended family. Have them tell you a story that you have never heard. (From tales told, students often discover traditions, generations, geography, and world history.) Be prepared to share this story with the class. Be descriptive. Practice telling it out loud using your voice and expression.

This assignment can extend into class work or future homework assignments for any age or subject matter. Tell or write the beginning, middle, and end of your story. Compare and contrast your story with a partner, small group, or entire class. Illustrate your story. Make up a different ending. Stories are made with words. What new vocabulary have you gained from the story? Create your own original story describing something interesting, exciting, or unusual. When imagination flows, it can lead to script writing, play acting, puppetry, and storytelling.

TESTING

I heard the words coming out of my own mouth when I was giving a talk in Japan, "Test scores can be ten points higher!" I was in the throes of a speech on self-esteem, making the point that when children feel good about themselves, everything is better. With a positive attitude and confidence, students do attain greater success

My students can't wait to take "those" tests! The reason? We have an agreement: if they test all morning, the afternoon is filled with excitement and surprises. Popcorn popping has an enticing smell, sound effects, and a taste that most everyone enjoys. Sometimes I combine it with a fun movie or video that is relaxing and reinforces our current or future studies. Once, I borrowed a microwave and bought special cornhusks that the popcorn actually pops off of before your very eyes. We were all mesmerized, an entire class silently watching flying popcorn kernels. (Sure took our minds off of testing that day!) Descriptive poetry and stories followed that included the five senses as well as happy students (and even buttered-stained papers from their busy fingers). When their writings were polished and perfected, illustrations and cartoon bubbling enhanced their works.

Homework during test week? Oh yes! The students (at any age) need to be reminded to wear comfortable clothes, have a good night's sleep, and to bring a yummy, healthy snack and a positive attitude. When children are encouraged to always try their best, this is just a "given" in the testing environment.

I give "homework" during test week to parent helpers and community volunteers. (They get an A for spending an afternoon with us after testing.) Some have brought a favorite story to read to the children and to dialogue about after. Once they brought in old potato sacks and pillow cases and the children participated in relay races, including three-legged races. For math, they logged the results with tallies, comparing the outcomes of races as well as team standings just for fun. Because we took this activity outside, it was a great release for children to move, run, and cheer. Visual, too, was the counting of watermelon seeds as we sliced the watermelon and discussed that testing is really not so bad after all.

I always hear so many negative stories about testing. (My least favorite thing is the frustration that I cannot help in any way and I tell the children that.) I decided to take my positive test reinforcement a step further to reach an entire school. As we all know, test doors are closed when the time clock begins. (Tardies don't make it in the door.) A system was set up for teachers to keep a record of which students were on time every day of testing and maintained a positive attitude. (Parent-documented illness was recognized if the child completed all of the necessary make-up tests.) That year, children throughout the entire school who accomplished the tasks were invited to a party that included a "real movie" and popcorn. What a novelty it was for children to interact and see a movie at school. The popcorn left on the floor was a true indication of a successful activity embraced by all participants.

Testing at my school has now become a celebration! This year, we drafted a colorful redeemable ticket. It has squares on it indicating each specific test included in the required test booklet and process. (Different colors are used as grade level and test sections varied.) All a teacher had to do was to mark the square at the completion of each test section and day (providing the student arrived on time and maintained a positive attitude). Tests make-ups have lessened, tardies have diminished, and you no longer hear the anti-test discussions among students, thus alleviating a lot of the stress

Testing throughout the country is inevitable and an annual occurrence. Using my premise of always finding something positive, a school can benefit from smooth testing and reaching a common goal together. This year, the party was outside on a grassy area by the playground. Those proud students holding their tickets of admission entered an afternoon of exciting activities. Spaghetti and pizza were donated and served, games were played, and I led the Macarena for all to participate and enjoy. The music played out of large speakers easily in earshot of such a large area, including lots of rhythm and variety. Many children in our school had never before had the opportunity to dance with "a real-live DJ." Thank you to our wonderful DJ, Chris Boucher, who selflessly donated his time to put the perfect touch and finale to testing! As hundreds of children were leaving the successful celebration and party, I overheard their similar conversations and complaints, "Why is testing only once a year?"

16

ENERGY, ENTHUSIASM, AND SPONTANEITY

I think the secret recipe for successful teaching includes only a few essential ingredients: flexibility, dedication, being open and positive, and a sense of humor (being able to laugh and enjoy). Also knowing that anything can and does happen! Mix these elements together along with energy, enthusiasm, and spontaneity. Student learning will soar while you are fulfilled beyond words. The two unusual experiences below include all of the above.

STORY ONE: BEGINNING OF A VACATION

My class of second, third, and fourth grade was in the middle of a thematic study surrounding science. Our focus, as we left for winter break, was on reptiles. Because I am always thinking of something extra to motivate my students, it is not unusual that I was inspired while on a family reunion trip to Mexico. I saw someone wearing a colorful, funny hat that was an alligator with lots of big teeth. It especially caught my eye since the math concept of bigger than (>) and less than (<) is always such a struggle for elementary students to understand. We talk about "alligator teeth" because if you draw teeth around numbers, an alligator would "eat" the bigger number indicating which way the sign goes. I was supposed to be relaxing, vacationing, and not thinking about school. (We all know how that goes.) Though the vendor would not bargain, I had to have one. (Spending our own money on school materials—that is something we just . . . do!) I overpaid and came home with an alligator hat for the visual learners. Some of my students were so excited with my hat and story that they made their own out of paper plates and scrap materials. Believe it or not, I wore my hat for math class and miraculously all of the students became proficient in this difficult math skill.

STORY TWO: LATER IN VACATION

We had cruised to ports in Mexico and were walking in another quaint city. I saw a vendor wearing an enormous, floppy, frog hat! Oh, oh! It aroused my interest so I decided it would capture my students too. It had large, bulging bright white eyes, a huge red tongue, and was bright green. To motivate my students, I purchased one giant green frog hat. I carried it as I continued sightseeing and lessons for every subject imaginable began running through my mind.

So, I decided to find the vendor again and get a few of these hats for a small learning group to do something with. Carrying seven and proud of my accomplishment, I went about my day. It was later that an idea came to me! The 100th day would be approaching when school resumed and we usually do a 100th-day presentation for the parents (and school) with an unexpected twist or theme. I used my math skills (my Spanish is very minimal) but I negotiated—and purchased—twenty-five frog hats and had the entire program in my mind. The vendor cleverly connected the hats with a rope going through them, almost like sausages or balloons all tied together.

My hair and complexion are dark, I was tanned, and there I stood in the middle of a city of international tourists in Mexico with twenty-five amazing frog hats. Because I am not quite 5'2", the "amazing" must have been the sight of me, surrounded by frogs on a hot day in Mexico. The next thing I knew, people were bargaining with me to buy frog hats! At first, I didn't really comprehend what was happening. Sometimes people require an extra moment to gather their thoughts and comprehend. When I said "No," more people surrounded me, talking a mile a minute in languages I did not understand. (And how do I convey to them that I just bought twenty-five frog hats for myself?) Those moments could have won the prize for what teachers do for their students! My class had the best 100th-day celebration and the creative stories flowed. We finished our science studies, but somehow math dominated when we began to count, tally, graph, and record eyes, frogs, hands, feet, toes, fingers, and tongues.

Little extras you give to your students incorporate who you are as well as transforming learning into an everyday special experience. I know, when I reflect on walking up that gangplank to embark on the cruise ship with those amazing frog hats, the amusement I brought to all who watched. Imagine the room steward seeing all of those frogs when he entered my small cabin. And you know what? The vendor was right. Those large bulging eyes were phosphorescent. I knew when I woke up in the middle of the night and fifty eyes were staring at me!

Frog hats.

EXCITEMENT

I walked into the classroom one morning and there it was—a large jar draped with a colorful cloth and a sign saying, "Don't touch." Curious? Of course I was and so were all of the students. We followed directions and didn't even take a glimpse until the appropriate time. The creative student instructed us to guess after she gave quite unusual and challenging clues. "There are so many. Most of them move. You will never guess!"

How right she was because no one could have possibly guessed. She did, however, reconfirm my philosophy that stimulating students takes

them steps "beyond." Heather, now a teenager who still smiles with recollection shared:

> In the second grade, my teacher brought in a
> huge jar full of jelly beans as a project. We
> had been learning estimation and the idea was
> for the class to estimate how many jelly beans
> were in the jar. After someone guessed the
> closest amount, Ms. Gail gave us the opportu-
> nity to bring in a jar of something for the class
> to estimate. So students started bringing in
> jars of marbles, candy, and stuff that was all
> the same. When it was my turn to fill the jar,
> I wanted to be new and creative. So I got the idea for bringing in a jar of
> more than 3,000 live ladybugs. No one in my class was able to guess even
> close to the exact number of ladybugs, so we took them to other classes.
> It was a sixth-grade boy who did finally guess the right amount. I let the
> ladybugs go in my backyard. You'll be happy to know we now have no
> aphids in our yard!

Estimating is a math process that develops as students gain an understanding of numbers and what they represent. It seems that the better
children estimate, the better their large-number recognition and understanding. The concept of math accuracy and understanding is also applied in real, day-to-day life.

I keep a large jar in the classroom. I fill it with different things, such
as paper clips, cotton balls, gumdrops, erasers and buttons. Students use
a form to record specific data. They are asked to guesstimate the number of items in the jar. After all have guessed, the number of objects is
written on the board. How close did they get? It is then that students
are asked to self-correct to indicate if their guess was more than or less
than the actual number. What is the difference? By how many? Students
discover accuracy, place value, estimation, and a better understanding of
number representation. Errors and miss-estimations count too! (Let
them see your guesses, especially the wrong ones.) If students keep an
accumulative record of their guesses, you can observe their increase in
math skills. Guessing becomes more "in the ballgame" and the differences are calculated with more accuracy and ease. You might want to in-

clude students in filling the jar. Rules need to be established to implement this. The first is the word *secret* so that the correct number of items is revealed to no one. If items are brought from home, guidelines also need to be established. It helps to require the answer to be written on a piece of paper to be hidden inside the lid. That is something I have needed countless times! Yes, you can divide objects into tens, hundreds, and thousands to find answers, but time sometimes is of the essence.

When I first challenged my students with jelly beans, I learned that they come in every size, color, and brand. First, the number of jelly beans was guessed. Next, students sorted by colors and recorded pertinent data. Comparisons came next of jelly beans, classmates, and peer groups that were tallied and graphed. Packages, contents, and even weight were examined and analyzed. This is a valuable tool to encourage student writing about their guesses and findings. Objects in the jar vary greatly and many of those become a story in themselves!

Of course, the students had the opportunity to eat the jelly beans and taste tests naturally occurred. Even figuring out favorite, familiar, different tastes from combinations of jelly beans! I am a "health food person" and actually don't like sweets. Enough jelly beans already, I thought, and I never should have said it but I did—"No more jelly beans! There can't possibly be any other kind!" (Always watch what you say!)

It was weeks later when I walked into my classroom and saw it! There was a large colorful surprise awaiting me and my students. I hope teachers truly appreciate all of the significant support staff at their sites! Mr. Augusto Garcia, our school custodian, not only accomplishes an amazing amount of work but also knows every student in the school. They love and appreciate him. And so did I until this very day. Mr. Garcia had been out of town and spotted packages of, shall we say, jelly beans with "problems." He purchased them and that is how this surprise happened to come to be. And so it was, we began all over again!

Dialogue began as these jelly beans had to be sorted quite differently. Some were adhered to each other, colors were faded, problems in sizing were distinct, and every imaginable mistake was represented in those packages. Charts were eagerly drawn depicting likes and differences. I didn't need to encourage stories because they were student generated, excellent and nonstop. Some great, best-ever poems were created as well. Even those who never got to see our problem jelly beans "saw" them in the vivid descriptions that the students created. Yes, and everyone also loved the tastes! The outside appearance didn't dictate what was on the inside! Thank you, Mr. Garcia, for your extended lesson. We loved the jelly beans with "problems" just as we accept each student for his or her diverse differences.

AND EVEN ... MORE?

To challenge students further, give them a "simple" assignment to see how astute they are. How many doors did they walk past to get to your classroom? How many windows? How many doors are in the entire school? Windows? Doorknobs? Whatever "relevant data" you decide on. If it includes measuring (such as, are all the doors the same size?), include a lesson on accurate measuring and how to line the ruler up at zero. (Even older students are careless and their measurements are not always true to size.)

This assignment can change to: How many mailboxes in an apartment complex? On a street? How many doors in an apartment? House? Complex? Street? What are the addresses on a street? The largest number? Smallest? Odd? Even? One side of a street compared to the other? What do all the addresses on a street add up to?

Mathematical questions can be endless! What is the mileage of the family car (bus to get to school) on Monday? Compare that to Friday. Encourage students to devise an assignment. Somehow measurement and mastery of concepts become fun and work is also more complete.

MENUS

When you keep an ever-expanding collection of menus, your lessons are infinite! They come in every shape and size, including varied types of print and style, from fast foods to gourmet dining, and what a difference in food categories and prices! When the word is out to bring you menus, they will arrive from everywhere!

Reading skills are a focus when students read the varied selections of food. Categorize and sort the selections. Not only breakfast, lunch, and dinner, but ethnic too! What country does a food traditionally represent? Geographically, where is that country in relation to your location? How many different languages do the menus represent?

As menus arrive continuously, academic discoveries are endless. Students can keep a log recording foods they have ordered when going to a restaurant (or what they would order if they could go to a restaurant). How long did it take to get seated? Served? What did others in the party order? Favorite food? Don't forget price comparison! Specials?

Wonderful story starters originate from menus too. Write about a favorite meal. (Worst meal?) If I could go to any restaurant, I would go to (restaurant). The restaurant I never want to go back to is (named) because (reason). The funniest thing that ever happened to me at a restaurant is (fill in the blank). I like to eat out because (reason) or (I don't like to (blank) because (reason).

To build a "restaurant" in your classroom, all you need is a table and some menus (or encourage students to use their imagination in making a "restaurant"). The top of a painted refrigerator box placed in a corner area did just fine for us. Menus can be from your collection or creatively made by the students. It is a great assignment for students to construct an original menu. If the options are open, what fun they have designing their menus.

Math options are amazing and can be challenging for any level of students:

- A list of what to order for carryout.
- The addition of a pretend restaurant check. Tip? Tax? Discount coupons? Half portions?
- Given five things to order, what is the amount of the meal?
- Given $10, what could be ordered to come closest to that amount?
- Plan a party for twenty people. Spending $300 maximum, plan the menu. (Would the cost be different for take-out to have the party at home or at the park?)
- Give comparison costs of the same entrée at different restaurants.
- If you could order one of everything that you want, make a list of your cravings. Estimate what the cost of ordering these foods would be. How close was your estimation? Calculate the difference.

I must confess that after completing menu math one day and reading the stories that the students started, I was hungry! Very hungry!! If you teach your students how to incorporate vivid descriptive adjectives in their writings, you'll be hungry too. No, I couldn't order everything, but that night I had a cheese enchilada and chili rellanos. I think it was the best ever—and probably tasted so good because I was so proud of the writing style that my students were already achieving long before I had expected them to.

If you contact local restaurants (have students write letters?), you can somehow make a contact to take your students somewhere. Then your lessons can involve anticipating the cost for your outing. Have a fundraiser to earn the money to go (Bake sale? Garage sale?). Begin adding the monies earned. How much more is needed? And if you do go, include lessons on the skills of correct letter writing to show student appreciation.

Because of my experience as a Fulbright Memorial Scholar to Japan, my students were immersed in the study of Japan. The opportunity was extended to my class to visit and dine at a local Japanese restaurant. (Thank you, Hiyama!) In preparation, we studied the traditional foods of the country. We discussed likes and differences, what tastes and textures we would encounter, and how it would be presented. When the big day came, we walked there together. The students proudly carried a large colorful flag they had made as a class project. On it was *Arigato* (thank you), written by each of the children next to their names. The flag waved, as together we walked the short distance to the restaurant where we presented it upon our arrival. The newspaper covered our special and tasty luncheon. It was not only exciting for the students to appear in the newspaper but also the restaurant that was so gracious to have all of us was acknowledged.

Upon returning to school, we made a collective list of all of the foods, tastes, talk, and the overall experience. The next day, students were able to begin illustrations and stories that developed into their amazing books about an extraordinary and memorable day.

MONEY COMPARISON

Money is stimulating in itself, simply because it is money. Students are fascinated with the differences in international money. (Do your students know about the pound, franc, yen, peso, peseta, lira, mark, and different dollars?) The bills of every country and denomination are so different. The languages, pictures, and value seem unusual, are intriguing, and foster geography, history, and world studies.

For a class assignment, ask students to record a written description of what type of an original dollar bill they might design. What country would it be from? What would it look like? When their writing is skillfully accomplished, have them make their dollar bill accordingly. First, we asked teachers and students from other classes to match the description with the coordinating dollar bills. Those that were well written were matched immediately. Others revised their work on their own so that they too could have their original "money" more easily recognized.

The next step was to remake the dollar bill, only this time on a large piece of butcher paper, and they were told they must include a hole in the middle. Into that hole, I mounted a picture of the child. What fun to see the money displayed with the distinguished students' photographs appearing on their "money!"

Don't forget to make a teacher dollar bill because for some reason that is always the favorite. Try designing a dollar bill to give out to students for special praise and recognition. I surprised my students with this once as a homework pass in lieu of a homework assignment of their choice. Just because! The more you give to your students, the stronger the rapport you create to teach the maximum skills that are a must for all. This, of course, generated one more idea. The whole class collectively constructed an enormous dollar bill to take up a classroom wall for display. In the middle of this masterpiece went the class picture taken on picture day, which I had blown up in size.

Another picture activity that has long been a fun favorite is to have each child make a life-size portrait of exactly what he or she looks like on picture day (or have them do it of partners). This direction needs to include the word exact, so it includes the clothes down to the shoelaces, color of hair, eyes, glasses, and every detail. When these are complete, they go to "rest" in the cupboard. We all know that school pictures take months to appear and when they do, be ready to share with your class—this is the moment that those creations come out of the cupboard. Arrange them somewhere in the classroom in the exact order of how they appear in the class picture. See if their drawings do match. Are they even close? Whatever, this is the type of experience that when children share, you are creating camaraderie and a "family" right in your class!

ENERGY

Travel is "in my blood." (It is all my mom's fault!) I save to share an adventure with her once a year, never knowing what encounters await us. In 1994 we went on a cruise in Europe. Of the 1,800 passengers, I was one of only seventeen who were not . . . shall we say, seniors? (We, thank goodness, found each other!) I always believe that out of negative comes positive and that things happen for a reason. Well, that was the actual week that the Macarena swept across Spain! I love to dance and the seventeen of us had ten days to master the new hand and movement dance with all sixteen beats of music. (The DJ also offered me the skill of figuring it out in double time.) Every room we walked into on that ship, the music would start playing just for us.

As soon as I got home, of course, my students had it perfected before America even knew what it was! I had recorded only the musical sounds with the catchy rhythm to capture student interest. Not only was the study of Spain and Europe enhanced but the music and dance taught progression, patterning, sequence, participation, and step-by-step directions. My students shared this in the school assembly as flamenco music was just beginning to be known across the globe. That is what learning is all about, the discovering and incorporating of new things.

ENTHUSIASM—ON APRIL FOOLS!

A "best" lesson is when the students (of any age) write a thorough and successful how-to essay—step-by-step appropriate progression, with a "right-on" topic sentence and a dynamic conclusion too. It is part of a lesson (I think my only one) that I teach year after year, entitled "How to Make a Sponge Cake."

I will walk you through the steps:

1. Buy a real sponge (any size, depending on . . . whatever your want).
2. Make (get) the frosting (most chocolatey aroma possible).
3. Spread the gooey (must be enticing) frosting in thick layers so it peaks and appeals.
4. Use the teacher talent that is a prerequisite in our profession (that of keeping a straight face even if you feel like you are going to burst!).
5. Before you demonstrate this lesson, you might first pull it on your students. And then, of course, deliver the finished product to the teachers' room. (It could be a whole chapter in itself!) Bring life to the teachers' room. (You know what I mean!)
6. If you assign this for "homework," that connection will be there when students have a parent help them pull this on someone for April Fools!

Editing this batch of papers is ecstatic. You will laugh through each one!

While on the subject of April Fools, following directions is an appropriate lesson for every student. Just tell them, "Today, we are having a test. We will practice silence in the classroom and correctly following every direction." Give them a print-out that appears to be an "official" test! The first direction must be "Do none of the directions below. Turn over your paper and draw me a picture of your desire." Watch as three-fourths of your students complete every imaginable question: Mother's maiden name. Address. Age. And so on, maybe twenty of your choices. They will all (every one of them) give to you . . . incredulous looks when the last line says "April Fools!"

POSITIVE ENERGY

Young Matt Volk has coached football at the high school and college levels. He found

> that the positive and trusting attitude is the only way to go. If you believe in a person, truly, and support them, they will succeed! I tell football players

Matt Volk in first grade.

that to be successful you have to play with love in your heart. I know, love and football don't go in the same sentence. If you truly love what you do you will be successful. It will drive you to learn, work hard, and win! That same attitude will travel over into any part of your life whether it is teaching, football, plumbing, or anything you do. If teachers can teach with the same love in their hearts, I believe they can affect a young person's life more than most people think. That love will drive them to learn more about what they teach, who they teach, and how they teach, which can only mean success for both the student and teacher.

Matt Volk:
college graduation.

STUDENT SPONTANEITY?

Irene was nine and that look on her face clearly told me that she could do no more. So, I announced to the class that they could use anything in the room to create something original. Extensive testing had just ended and the students needed a release that was also meaningful. Before I even knew what was happening, she had created the most magnificent designer creation imaginable! Irene had gathered paper, string, and scrap materials of every color and texture possible. She cut, glued, and stapled them together. On her! What she modeled could have appeared in a fashion window and been featured as a designer "one of a kind."

Irene Bavaro: creative!

Once, a refrigerator occupied the big box that is now a yellow "treasure chest" in the corner of my room and a cherished item among my educational materials. Filled with scraps of things that might be classified as junk, these treasures come alive in hands-on learning projects enhancing instruction in every academic area. The self-expression of children making new inventions is incomprehensible. I incorporate this in teaching because it is enticing and helps some to thrive. That box lets students know that it is safe to discover their own ideas.

Allow students to enrich your curriculum and extend the learning process. Designate a time, day, special assignment, and challenge them to create. Choices give them ownership and power. Discovery yields learning while investigating non-stop possibilities. Watch them become engrossed. Interesting collages have become masterpieces. Creative writing about their creations is excellent because the entire concept is something they have originated. (Irene even developed written advertisements, including illustrations depicting her talent.)

Sometimes these lessons and exciting explorations remain a part of their memory banks for years to come!

HAVING A BAD DAY?

Everyone has one. This one is called "Teacher Spontaneity—November 7, 2002."

Early this morning as I was putting the finishing touches on this manuscript, the text on my computer disappeared before my very eyes. Scared and disappointed, a smile came over me because I had backed up my book on discs only four days ago.

I drove to school on this, the first rainy day of the year in sunny California. I discovered my classroom roof leaking all over the materials I had prepared for the day. A parent volunteer unexpectedly couldn't come. A bird flew in through the open doorway and perched on a wire where student artwork was being displayed.

It is a new procedure to take a cafeteria count; I did, sent it in, and "the" day began. The classroom phone, however, interrupted with a continuous loud ring. The call was to inform me that my cafeteria count was blank. I could only laugh out loud realizing that the raindrops had erased the tally marks.

You can well imagine the children's excitement and noise level, and it was only 9:21 A.M. So together we made the choice to have a great day. It is all . . . attitude! We watched the gray clouds turn purple and then a colorful rainbow lit up the sky. I encouraged descriptive writings about these mishaps that began to flow as students created cartoons, illustrations, short sentences, essays, and original books about this day—a day that normally would be every teacher's nightmare became this teacher's dream because every student was actively engaged.

⓱

THE CONNECTION

They gave me my million-dollar reward as an educator! With a teehee and glee in their bright, gleaming eyes, twenty-three cuties of every shape and size looked up to me with eager anticipation as they presented me with a smooth, twisted, shiny, unusual, beige twig that they had secretly searched for on the beach. We shared the moment and I learned that they had planned it as their goal of that day, finding me a real "magic wand."

Often, I am asked what I need to help me in my many endeavors. My response is always "just a magic wand" because there is magic in the twists and turns that spin throughout relating to children. It includes excitement that is genuinely felt from the tips of my toes and throughout my very soul and being. I never know which way any new day will go. The children take me to such new heights with their open eyes, wonderment, innocence, and curiosity. When I took my very first step as a teacher, it became apparent that teaching is a real-life experience, intertwining each and every second. No two days or moments are ever the same.

We went to the beach to meet our pen pals and because we were studying the environment and natural interdependence of nature. Students from two cities, an hour away, corresponded throughout the school year. Pen pals connected through their writings, which included many interesting questions and answers. As a teacher, it was rewarding to watch the development of written language and the connection and bonding of children. If you can incorporate a similar experience with your students, it builds anticipation as well as an eagerness to write. When letters are received, students can't wait to read them. We have exchanged pictures as well as murals about the children and our studies. We have taped songs, favorites and originals, and enjoyed sending them.

The meeting is exciting, yet might cause some intimidation and worry, so I've created a remedy for that. Get a variety of wallpaper books donated. Have your students select a distinct piece of wallpaper pattern and cut it in half. This is the final correspondence and a surprise to send to the other class before the big day. As students first catch a glimpse of each other, it is only the matching wallpaper that they have to be concerned about. Once they've "matched," the rest is easy.

Part of the written assignments throughout the year included ongoing specific descriptions to the pen pal of things that they did *not* like to eat. This requires descriptive writing and focus on the facts received because the highlight of the meeting was making lunch for each other. (Whether illustrations or writings were used throughout the communication process, the reward for work well done was an enjoyable lunch to the students' liking.)

As we were packing up to leave, we discussed the joys of the day, which included connecting with new friends, beautiful weather, finding interesting shells, playing games, and merely being together in an out-of-school activity. The children discussed how special it was that we could share so much.

WHAT IS "CONNECTION?"

There are many special moments in life that are celebrations. In teaching, it is the chance to inspire students and to reach them. When you connect as a "real" person, trust becomes incorporated into your lesson plans. Add a touch of humor and remember, for some of your students, you are all they have. You could be the only constant in a student's life. The consistency of you being there each day is a lesson in itself. You are the one they know who will really listen and appreciate them for who they are, as you reveal the knowledge that will make a difference in their lives.

When you share, they know you care. Your influence teaches not only academic requirements but also the continued encouragement for success. Though they will challenge you, they are communicating. When they know you envision progress, students will find a way to do their best. For even when you are teaching, let them know that you are also always learning, too.

A CONNECTION MADE THE DIFFERENCE

The doorbell rang in my suite in Tokyo at 2 A.M. All alone in a foreign country, I couldn't imagine what it could be? I slowly opened the door and was handed a fax from my stu-dents in California with ques-tions about the fish market. "Do they have octopi?" (Also included was an original song written by a student about puffer fish!) I could only laugh out loud and didn't feel alone anymore because I felt such a strong "connection!"

Before I left home for Japan, everyone told me that going to the fish market in the middle of the night was a must. I told my students I would probably go there on Thursday. They were home in the midst of summer vacation and following my trip as best they could through my itinerary that we had studied together. (Of course, it was parent help that got that fax all the way to Tokyo, but I took it with me to the fish market at 3:00 A.M.) They gave me more than I could ever have asked for—the feeling of love and support when on a journey at the other end of the world.

It was my first time in a cab in Japan, which is an adventure in itself because the doors rapidly fly open automatically. I was half-awake in the middle of the night, and couldn't speak the language to tell exactly where I wanted to go. The student drawings in my hand became the map and my connection. They gave me the tool to find the fish market! What a great experience it was!

A MESSAGE

Someone once said to me, "How would it be if every child started school on their fifth birthday with a birthday cake as a celebratory beginning?" The idea of the positive first step into school sounded appealing to me yet every five-year-old is different. Every child is different! "Readiness" varies in every aspect of a young child. Some are called "late bloomers" and they will bloom. Children unfold as exceptional individuals when they are ready.

Jeff Mihaly in first grade.

Note students' idiosyncrasies as you pay attention to each of them. Increase your sensitivity as you understand their inner worlds and help them to feel understood. Establish your priorities because the expression "pick your battles" applies to teachers as well as parents. Something "little" that you can find a way to overlook is something "big" for a particular child.

One child (we've all had them) always doodled on his papers. He wasn't destroying school property and, actually, he wasn't interrupting the learning process of other students. As I approached the concept of neatness and responsibility with my class, I pondered over this. I had noticed that when he drew on his papers, he appeared to be listening to my every word. If I gave him "the look" and he stopped, his focus was anywhere but on me. So we came to an understanding: if his academic work was his best,

*Jeff Mihaly:
pursuing animation.*

then he could doodle. And, I have to tell you, that from that day on, despite his drawing, his work not only flourished but his attitude and outlook did, too.

Ten years later, I received this note from Jeff Mihaly (see front cover art):

When sitting at my desk, I would always have an urge to start drawing on anything that I could draw on. I wasn't able to sit there at my desk and concentrate on what I was being taught. I remember that I was nervous and used to worry about getting in trouble for not staying on task. The day I knew I would not get in trouble, I started to draw more and became more proud of my art. I began to be able to share my drawings with my classmates, be happy about them and not have to worry as much as I used to. Since I had gotten more inspiration, I would draw more. That led to improvement in my drawings and made me think about taking my art seriously. I am now accomplishing my goal in life to become an animator!

PUT THOUGHTS INTO THEIR HEADS

Over the years, some students have told me they were "born not to like math." Someone "afraid" of math? This begins the challenge of finding a way to connect even more!

Sometimes we have watched the numbers align on a digital clock. Together, we have gotten excited watching the clock say 1:11, 2:22, or 3:33. Have to begin somewhere! I always know on New Year's that wherever my past students of thirty-three years are, they will be watching the clock. Many stories have come to me how former students still "connect" with me, especially on 01:01:01:01:01 (January first, one minute, one second, after one o'clock to begin the year 2001.)

Demonstrate with creative activities and thoughts that math is a part of everyday life. Once with college students, I even used stoplights for an example. Students were assigned to go to a corner of their choice and figure the timing of the yellow, red, and green lights. Approximately how many cars were allotted per time slot? Compare to another intersection? What if there were no stoplights? Or no maps to indicate distances? Find something about you to connect in some way.

You might have students bring in similar products for comparison analysis. One company indicated on their packaging how many candies per ounce were in the package. After a lot of counting, tallying, and sticky hands, students discovered the company was wrong! For the experience of expressive written language, I sent the students' findings to the company. Students were delighted when a big package arrived one day with an abundant variety of candies and cookies. More significant, though, we saw that the company had changed the mathematical equivalent calculation on its new candy packaging.

Getting students to connect to learning is not only the beginning but also a method to the best end results you can possibly imagine.

WORLD FAMOUS MATHEMAGICIAN

You've probably been amazed if you've been lucky enough to see him make a guest appearance on television. I couldn't sleep for three nights after I saw him appear at the world-renowned Magic Castle in Hollywood. Not only did numbers come alive when he visited my school but for weeks after students were calculating what they used to call impossible sequential numbers and equations. Even the child who "hates math" mastered those times tables in an attempt to "beat the calculator!"

Some of the children were non-English speaking and others represented an array of math levels and ability, but he made a profound connection with each of our school's 580 students. To quote Arthur Benjamin, a professor at Harvey Mudd College:

> When I teach mathematics, I find that students respond best to material that is either relevant or elegant.
>
> I probably learned my most valuable teaching skills by doing magic shows for children's birthday parties when I was in high school. A good lecture should be structured so that it has an attention-getting introduction and a satisfying conclusion. To keep them interested throughout, it is good to have lots of audience participation and a sense of humor. (Benjamin 2002)

SHARE YOUR EXPERIENCES

Be a real human being! Relating to your students will capture even the
inattentive ones who can't wait to hear more. Through your experiences,
students learn how to listen and pay attention.
    Hailey explains:

Summer was two weeks away and Ms. Gail sent me to
the library. The books were almost talking
to me so I checked out all the
books I found on elephants. I
suddenly liked them because
I read about how happy they
could be and they have feelings
just like me. So the whole class
including the teacher began to read
and talk about elephants and then vacation began.

    The next thing I knew Ms. Gail was unexpectedly invited to Thailand
and was in elephant school. (Heaven to her!) She called and told us that
the new baby elephants had red hair and would lay down under a baby
blanket. It made me interested in something new and exciting. Learning
can just keep happening even when you least expect it.

Adrian looked forward to my "stories" and came back to share:

When you tell stories, you let me into your world. Even a short one is exciting and I can't wait for the next. I start to think of ideas of my own and
stories I want to tell. You taught me that almost anything can be a story
and often I think about what to tell or write next. You communicate with
me and I open up to communicate more of me. You told me little secrets
and then I wanted to know everything you had to say! Not many teachers
have dressed up in a gorilla outfit and surprised the Cub Scout campout!
How funny that when you were little you took the labels off of all of the
cans in your kitchen cupboards! If all teachers told little stories, the material they are teaching might be listened to more by people just like me!

The first day, he ran away from the school office. The second day, this
interesting child entered my class and said, "I hate school! Nobody can

make me do a thing. I wish school was
never invented!" The next thing we knew,
he wouldn't go to recess because he was
having so much fun. Days went by and
this child who could or would do nothing
discovered Russia.

To quote John: "Russia was the only
thing that made me start liking school.
Books became my friends and I couldn't
stop reading. Then I wouldn't stop writing. I finally had something to talk to people about and even made friends. I am
still fascinated about Russia and have
since made many other new discoveries."

John Mazin: wearing Russian hat.

John wasn't a "problem," just a child with a fabulous mind needing
challenge and enrichment. When I found that spark about Russia, I
learned along with John. An unexpected opportunity came about and
soon I was off to Russia! Thank you, Viking River Cruises, for making
history come alive and meaningful. I suddenly found myself sitting in
the Hermitage Theatre. It was hard to believe it when I was actually
watching the Russian Ballet.

As I looked out the window of a public bus, I saw a man wearing a
Russian military hat with Russian pins all over it. I got off the bus and
followed the man with the hat. We talked as much as two people can
who don't speak the same language. Everyone on that bus watched and
listened as I counted out rubles in an attempt to actually buy that hat.
And I did! I returned to the bus quite satisfied and everyone cheered. I
wish I spoke the language to explain how I felt. John had made a difference in my trip. I could hardly wait to get home and discuss what Russia is really like and to give him the hat!

CHILDREN VALUE YOUR CONNECTION

The connection with your "children" lasts for a lifetime.
Cindy Cross recalls:

Last summer, I was going through some boxes and came across some old school papers with a familiar happy face on them. I remembered that the happy face meant I had done well. Getting the happy face made me want to do better so I could get them all the time. It made me go that extra step to reach my goal. Something as simple as a happy face showed I was recognized for doing my best. Doing your best, that's what is important in life! I don't get happy faces now but when someone tells me I did well, then I try to do better each time to reach that goal.

Cindy Cross: early years.

Steve, a seven-year-old, wrote: "My teacher and I connect because we both smile and we are both happy. My teacher and I connect because I like the wonderful things she teaches."

Nine-year-old Micaela thought future teachers should know that connecting is important:

1. You both can find out stuff you didn't know before.
2. You can learn a *lot* more.
3. You can communicate with each other.
4. You'll be more prepared.
5. You can have a circle
6. You can get out your animosity.
7. You can be more companionable.
8. You can ask questions that you can't ask anyone else but *your* teacher.
9. You can find out great and horrible facts that you should know.

SSgt Cynthia Cross.

Eight-year-old Cathy told me that connecting is the most important thing she has learned.

Connections are how people communicate with each other. If you didn't have a connection with someone, then you wouldn't be able to communicate in an open way. Connecting can be positive or negative. Some people connect in a bad way. If two people didn't have a connection, they might not be able to understand each other. Connections are something that people do all the time. They may not even know that they are doing it. Everybody loves connecting in a positive way because it helps to bring the world closer together. I love connecting with my teacher because it helps me to learn.

MYSTIFICATION

I believe in understanding that each child is truly unique and special. Children bring with them their dreams and what energizes them as an individual. Each student is on a journey. For many, it is yet to be discovered, but there are those few with a strong passion from an early age. As educators, it is our hope to diversify a student's exposure and to open his or her eyes to as many avenues as possible.

Tristen, however, was a young girl who drew pictures of toe shoes and tutus, counted as if she was at a ballet bar, and always wrote about dance. Though I introduced her to diverse topics and experiences, I realized that her passion was far too strong for me to interfere. Every student has his or her "needs" and her pictures became beautiful illustrations for fluid stories about dance. It was through her that I learned about the history of dance and rich information about cultures and world traditions.

Tristen Gire in first grade.

I almost felt her rhythm and watched her "dance" as she walked from place to place in the classroom. I was overwhelmed with her first dance performance for the entire school. (None of us wanted it to end.) After that, we were not only mystified but we all knew! Tristen was a natural and dance was her passion and world.

Tristen: prima ballerina.

To quote Tristen Gire today:

> From the moment I set eyes on the beautiful ballerinas through the window at our local dance studio, I knew I wanted to be just like them. My mom says I was tiptoeing around in my walker before I was crawling. I guess that explains why dancing has been my whole life since before I can remember. It is who I am. If someone were to ask who Tristen is, they would get a response similar to: "Oh, she's that little blonde dancing girl." Dance was what I loved and the harder I worked, the better I became, and the better I became, the more I grew to love it. It was a vicious cycle that shaped my whole life. Similar to any sport, there were times of encouragement and times of pressure. But as long as my tutu kept getting bigger and more elaborate, my determination kept growing.

My students dreamed of going to the Civic Arts Theater to see the Nutcracker. In class, we had discussed the rigorous practicing and determination of dancers. In preparation, we had thoroughly reviewed the story and, as they watched the ballet, they were intrigued. They took it all in—the music, costumes, scenery, and the motion of dance! The best part was the excitement that they were going to meet a real prima ballerina! As theatergoers left the theater, we waited in the foyer.

Leaning against a pole, the young woman with a radiant smile began speaking to my students. She was confident, genuinely interested in them, and eager to meet them. Suddenly, "Who are you?" shouted out my usually quiet student who had been anticipating this special moment. It was then that the children became aware that even prima ballerinas wear torn, comfortable sweats because it truly was the ballerina, Tristen, happy to answer questions and share her life passion of dance.

> As a youth I went across the country training as a ballerina in New York and San Francisco. Now I am a dance major at the University of California in Irvine. My experiences here have been amazing, including touring to Los Angeles and New York and performing on stage an average of five times a year. It's funny to look back and see all I went through to become what I am today. Here I am, starring the lead role in the Nutcracker, signing autographs for little girls just like me ten years ago. The sparkle in their eyes when they spoke to me reminded me just what it feels like to have a heart full of dreams. I know firsthand that dreaming and a little bit

of determination will get you a long way. My experience of becoming what I wanted to be has made me a stronger person than if I had chosen the easy road. I am grateful for everything I went through, and if my life inspired others along the way, then all the better.

A VIDEO FELL OUT OF THE CUPBOARD

It had no label on it and since I rarely play any video, the students urged me to play it. It was a program of sequence, song, and original plays from students seven years earlier. Not only was this a novelty but it was perfect timing: we were in the midst of perfecting our presentation of original puppet shows and dance. As they watched, my students took careful note of voice projection, audience presence, eye contact, and all of those lessons that seeing is better than me telling.

We specifically discussed one boy, B.J., smiling at us on the video because I was giving a "teacher example" of how everyone can be a success! Some who had older siblings remembered him as the boy who didn't speak English and was always in trouble. We talked about how he had learned English, grasped a positive attitude, and developed a love of learning. The valuable discussion that transpired reconfirmed the message

It couldn't have been scripted any better when an amazing thing happened! Standing in the open doorway, on roller blades, was a tall young man. He came from 100 miles away, a relative brought him to say "hi" as he was about to start high school. I couldn't believe my eyes as we hugged and I kept saying, "B.J., we just watched you on video." To him, that made no sense at all until the children told him what had happened. Though it was seven years later, he began to recite his parts from memory while I got out the video, again, to share with him.

His English now was excellent, as was his confidence, and B.J. stayed for the day blending in with the children. Because they had just heard my story

B.J. Torres returns to visit.

about how B.J. had developed his English through math manipulatives and flashcards, who would have ever thought he would be there in person to demonstrate! I flashed through my memory of when B.J. used to withdraw from any kind of oral experience as I watched him lead math activities and explain to the students how to remember math facts. (All those little secrets and practice, he recalled, had paid off.)

He also gave me a note: "When I went to your class, I got better grades because you were not so strict, like other teachers. You helped me in many ways. The hands-on teaching always helped me to understand the work. Being able to express myself, I felt better about myself and felt important in the class. We learned from our problems and each other, and now have good lasting friendships."

LEAVE IT TO THEM!

There are always those moments when a teacher could use a surprise. Eight-year-old Charlene decided it was time to share her unique and original creation with me. With a bursting smile and a giggle, too, she showed me an old piece of paper. On it were the grapes from a lesson we had completed about six weeks ago. (We had tasted, compared, journaled, and graphed the characteristics of three types of grapes—colors, flavors, likes, and differences.) Amazingly, what was now before me were raisins! The grapes had been secretly taped and saved on her paper. We now had three different raisins: one yellow, one black, and one purple. (To quote Charlene: "Puffy, shiny, one smushed, one halfway smushed, and one very perfect big one.") I don't use the word "perfect" in teaching because we do our best, but this grape had become as perfect as a raisin could possibly be. Science prevailed and an unexpected lesson came about.

OTHERS CAN CONNECT WITH YOUR STUDENTS

With a long, swiftly wagging tail and a spirited bounce in the gait, a black lab puppy appeared out of nowhere and began to follow us. Twenty students and I were on a walking trip and this was the last thing I needed.

Next to us, on a large street in the center of town, a school bus stopped and the door opened automatically. The puppy apparently thought that this was an invitation and proceeded to bound onto the bus. When the driver let it know that the bus was not where it was supposed to be, it ran off the bus and the dog adopted me. Worried about this puppy nipping a child, but with no choice but to continue, we all walked together until the puppy decided to run into the traffic.

Jade Rosenbloom: "hero" with Angel.

Visions of the worst flashed before my eyes. My concern was the safety of my students and I was afraid they would follow the dog into the busy street. We froze and Jade, one of my students, let out a piercing scream. A major intersection came to a halt. The puppy ran back to join our group, and in my thoughts, this all seemed like a storybook tale.

Safe back at school, the family of the dog was called, and our story had a happy ending. It didn't end though! The next day, a huge container of chocolate chip cookies was delivered to the school along with a personal note. That note meant more to my students than anything! (The connecting of someone reaching out to us!) We copied the note for each child to take home and blew it up to post in our window for all to share.

Dear Ms. Gail's Class,

My name is Mrs. Levin. I am Angel's Mommy. I am writing this letter to let you all know how much Mr. Levin and I appreciate how you saved our baby, Angel. Angel is very special to us. We don't have children, just Angel and Slinky the cat (both were adopted through an Animal Rescue). Angel went to work with her daddy yesterday, and somehow got out of the yard where she plays. Her daddy had already been looking for her for some time. I am so happy too that Angel had her tags on. I called our house and your message was on our machine. If not for your brave class, Angel could have been hurt or put in a place where she would have been very sad. I am so thankful for all of your help. Angel is home now and asleep in her bed with her brother, Slinky.

Again, thank you and sincerely,

Mr. and Mrs. Levin and Angel

Every time you connect is a valuable teaching tool. This connection was a strong element that none of us will ever forget. Sharing the emotions of a last day of school, my students had an unexpected surprise that was "like the frosting on the cake" for our school year. Angel and her family were waiting in the front of the school to thank us once again and to wish us a special summer and everyday. We sat on the lawn and took pictures with Angel and what a beautiful way for summer to begin!

18

PARENT INVOLVEMENT

Next to my home phone sits a class roster because one never knows when you might just need it! How exciting it is for a parent to receive a phone call from the teacher regarding a child's special accomplishment on an extraordinary day. Imagine the pride a child feels when they know that their teacher has noticed.

It takes only a few extra minutes to acknowledge a child's success, yet that time can lead to diminished disciplinary problems. That positive direction creates awareness for parents and children. When all are informed, there are no surprises. When the positives (no matter how small) are stressed, children begin to feel more confident.

I can't even count how many times I've "sent a child to the principal" (an understanding one) for new growth in academic areas or for increased listening skills, better peer relationships, or for extended effort. There is always "good" to be found in every student. Sometimes you wonder . . . but when you dedicate yourself to finding something good, new doors open for everyone. In the event you are the first teacher to discuss the special qualities in a certain child, negative stories the parents (and child) might share with you can be mind-boggling.

Establishing rapport with the parents early on has an effect on the parent-teacher relationship. Parents can become your best allies. When they know that you believe in their child, they will give you their max. The stages a child goes through, the good and the bad can easily be discussed in a working relationship between parents and teacher. They know that your constructive comments will help their child's development in the long run. Positive encouragement is always an added plus. Nothing will help a child more than the cooperation of the parents, teacher, and principal.

I suggest beginning the school year with two types of questionnaires. One is for parents to have the opportunity to tell you about their child. I find that virtually all parents want the best for their children. Do not ask necessarily for strengths, weaknesses, or ability levels, but rather information that they think will help you to better relate and know their child!

How do you utilize parents? Many have expertise and knowledge that can enhance your teaching. You are the educational experts and the parents want to follow your lead. Parent-teacher collaboration fosters learning and nurtures growth for the children. Parent involvement is beneficial to the child, class, parent, and teacher. Because of this, the second questionnaire that I recommend is designed to get the parents involved in your educational program. Survey their strengths, and indicate your goal to work together! What attributes (occupational skills or hobbies) can they bring to your classroom? Always remember that their kids are your kids! (For how many hours a day?) Sometimes parents share something not only with a class of students but also with their own children!

(Maybe a skill or idea they have not had time to discuss at home.) I find, too, that parent volunteers often further inspire your students and bring out other avenues to take.

The question is always raised of how to handle varied learning styles and individual student needs. When appropriate work is being done, there is less negativity. Children do not have to face frustration or want to give up. Given realistic work, progress becomes immeasurable. A parent in the classroom can work with a small group of students, help log in homework, record book numbers, read a special story, ask comprehension questions, or help with something as simple as cursive guidance. (That sure helped me, being left-handed. I'll always remember the day I discovered some right handed children writing just like me!)

Assistance you ask for does not have to be only in the classroom. (Help can include making folders, phone calls, precutting materials for a project, proofreading grammar, and such.) Outside help not only includes the parents in the process of their child's education but also alleviates some teacher time to allow you to put your minutes into something else for your students.

To ensure communication, keep the parents informed on a regular basis! Send letters home stating your goals and classroom activities. Ask for ideas! In working with elementary children, create a parent information board where you can display a regularly updated class calendar as well as teacher thoughts that you want to share. When parents are well informed and feel you have nothing to hide, they feel more comfortable, welcome, and supportive.

When you interact and dialogue with the parents, skills you use in teaching often begin to apply at home (such as organization, problem solving, and communication). Parents are a support system for their children. Not to "do" homework, but to dialogue and participate, sharing lives together. Everyone benefits because better learning enriches self-confidence.

Often parents ask what specifically they can do for their children. The simplest answers are often just the words to remind them of instrumental approaches, which can make a difference: Is continuous support being given? Help children to gain necessary confidence! There are many things that a child must do; the adults are best to only guide, encourage, and challenge them. Be consistent and encouraging. Motivate children and help them to develop a good attitude. Children need to acquire the principle of patience to truly reach for success and accomplishment. Encourage children to take risks and to trust their intuitive desires, because these can sometimes contribute to the course a child takes. Possibly the most important thing a parent can do is to listen to what their child is saying! Hear them and carefully think about their words and messages!

In *Pocket Coach to Parenthood*, Åsa Nelson-Odbäck states "Heart, caring joy, and commitment—these are the marks of a good player in the game of parenthood. Love is the name of the game, and winning the trust and closeness of your child is more rewarding than any other game there is to play" (Nelson-Odbäck 1997).

Sometimes when I sit in a parent-teacher conference, we laugh together and share dialogue because it is like "any other day." Keeping the parents informed and included reinforces everything you are doing in a timely manner. School and home communication builds as you work together. All of you—child, family, and teacher—can experience the giant (and baby) steps as they are taken. Sharing is the valuable component in teaching that reaps the highest rewards. Talk to the students. It always amazes me how a student with consistent effort and determination will suddenly make a discovery or an accomplishment of a long-awaited goal. It is like someone turns on a light bulb! The most meaningful "reward" a student of any age can ever receive from any teacher is recognition, sharing the meaningful progress with genuine excitement.

Once a young child began "reading" for the first time. I stopped the class to recognize the glow an individual child was feeling. When you include circle and a "family-like" classroom atmosphere in your teaching, children are more inclined to share each other's momentous occasions. When it is immediate, it is truly a moment to remember.

I have also had a child use the school phone (or my cell phone) to call the parents. How appropriate for parents to hear a child's voice with a positive ring to it! "I just mastered my multiplication." "I read a story without having to sound out each word." "I practiced strategy and mastered a game of chess."

MEMORABLE PARENT "HELP" = UNFORGETTABLE!

A pilot flew over our school and photographed it. Next, he came in to help lead mapmaking and geography skill work. Students became enthralled with the idea that he flew the plane, which was instrumental in achieving concepts of mapping and direction, the compass rose, as well as height and altitude. New interests prevailed along with an extra dimension in teaching these skills. The students mapped out where they lived, places they had been (or wished to go) and the location of extended family members and friends. A linkage of writing skills and math data developed, including self-discovered comparisons, likes, and differences.

Scientists brought into the classroom the directions, materials, and hands-on activities regarding the actual making of DNA. This included the entire scientific process, hypothesis, and research. The extended discussions that followed were amazing. Another day, a scientist explained atoms, performing a factual demonstration using ping-pong balls (and Legos). One lesson on vacuum included expanding marshmallows to explain the concept of vacuum. The children watched as marshmallows got bigger and smaller before their very eyes.

Many times children have utilized the language and reading curriculum to create original scripts. Parents have helped them to evaluate and edit their masterpieces, sometimes even typing a working script to plan a "production," no matter how big or small. Students in the process of gaining confidence develop even more when they perform in front of peers, fellow classmates, or parents. Parents can help with the practice sessions, voice inflections, stage presentation, scenery, a compatible song, and even making invitations if the children decide to share their talent with others, which exhibits comprehensive mastery. Some of this "help" can even be done at home. The key is drawing out the imagination of children, which includes accidental creations and spontaneous works.

One parent indicated that he couldn't help when he told me, "No English, no time." I encouraged him to show up if he had even one free hour at any time. And he did! "No English," he reminded me and he successfully guided a few children who needed help with multiples of numbers using manipulatives!

Cooking is another area for appealing and related projects that volunteers enjoy helping with. Some of my "keeper" creative writing has been students writing a recipe book of "How Mom (whoever) Cooks (fill in blank)." Did you know a turkey weighs ninety pounds? It takes forty-nine minutes to cook? At 13 degrees? Did you know that freezing is at 300°C? Even older students don't have a concept of how many degrees to cook a turkey. For how long?

Students can have a firsthand opportunity to use and compare Fahrenheit and Centigrade degrees. The skill of measurement is something students seem to struggle with. For example, that 2/4 and 1/2 are really the same. "How can that be?" they always ask. But when they see it by doing the pouring and measuring themselves, they begin to not only understand the concept but also remember!

Sometimes I wonder about ESP. I guess in reality, it is caring parents as they get to know you as a teacher, a person. "Do you need any help?" These words can sound like music at times (or an answer to a prayer). It is often the day that something needs to be stapled and it just didn't get done. It has been help with a computer glitch when the computers are down and refuse to cooperate. One non-English parent poked her head in the door just to look. Through gestures, I found out she could sew. And it was she who helped a sewing project when I was feeling quite frustrated trying to help some older boys learn how to tie a knot before their sewing could even begin. She had the magic touch, an extra pair of hands, and was our hero that day.

Many teachers I know do not want any parents in the classroom. They want privacy and not any possibility of feeling intimidated. When a teacher is prepared, there really is nothing to hide when parents are involved. It is actually beneficial for parents to be "in the know" so they can be supportive. If you are lucky enough to have any parents who even show an interest, find a way to include them!

For those teachers who have no parent input or volunteers, it is still to your advantage to be warm and responsive when you see the parents. (They don't always need to have an "appointment.") If you are in a situation where you don't see the parents, your letters home can be done in a way to capture a little more interest. (Even if one more parent will take the extra moment to read what is going on at school, it's worth it.)

Encourage "too-busy parents" to sign up to come in—even if for only an hour here or there. When teaching Africa was a required component, I was in a quandary as to how to make it significant for my students. When you seek resources, you extend to students firsthand learning. I remember a parent telling me her schedule was too busy to get involved on a regular basis. It was one of those middle-of-the-night thoughts that came to me to ask this professional artist to spend a day in my classroom. After we dialogued about the possibilities, I stripped the walls in anticipation of a learning day to remember.

We put together an event, and now fourteen years later, Susan Perret recalls what transpired:

> I think the spectacle of working together on an art project combined with a sense of multimedia, gave the children an added feeling of excitement. The subject matter of Africa was colorful and I personally loved creating paintings/collages on Africa. The contrast of color, an exotic place, something new and not about our own country made for an exciting learning experience. Backed up by African music, the children came alive!
>
> I personally began a series of paintings on Africa. I loved the people and their lovely use of brilliant color. How wonderful that in some small way, as an artist, I could pass on that bubbly excitement to eager little minds. Thank you, Gail, for dedicating your career to enhancing the education, and actually being a key that activates the minds of our children. My three kids were set in motion by you and continue to be eager to learn.
>
> Today, because of our electronic age, our children are bombarded and tend to rely on the computer too much. What I think they need is another view of the world as well. One that can help them feel and experience a tactile sense of our world . . . it gives them an outlet to express their heart. We need to cultivate the poetry of life and begin to humanize our children and ourselves. This is a way to start our human race on a more sympathetic course towards life on Earth!

While the children turned our classroom into Africa, I personally learned masterful teaching techniques from a parent.

Another possibility is if a child has a grandparent nearby. Even just to read a favorite story is appropriate for any children. It is a different presentation, and the voice, the story, and the interpretation of another adult. Afterwards, I encourage oral comments and comprehension discussions about the outcome of the story, sequence, character traits, possibly a different ending, and author/book comparisons.

Some areas have senior citizen volunteers. In reality, this is of value to not only the students but the seniors as well. Students can get a little extra one-on-one learning, and possibly a skill to boost understanding, or that little push to forge ahead. Seniors bring their intuition and feel needed, important, and fulfilled. One shy senior quickly advised me the first day that she would only read with one child at a time in a quiet setting. Just as students grow, so did she! Eventually, she worked with a small group of children in an adult-directed literature circle. I often know "what day" it is because students look forward to a special volunteer. One senior volunteer helped to count jumps of fifth-grade students who had never learned to jump rope. Together, they took it to another level—complete with predictions, tallies, averages, and peer comparisons.

Another retired senior volunteer, Diane Simpson, states:

> Two young girls were assigned to me for one half hour, informal, one-to-one sessions once a week. This ultimately expanded to several girls and boys for many half-hour sessions. The children seemed most comfortable establishing this mutually respectful intergenerational relationship. This flowered by sharing stories of our experiences, our insights, our values, and each other. Each of the children could choose what they most wanted to do at each session—conversation, crafts, tutorial, practice reading and comprehension, writing stories, planning the next session, spelling bees, and even showing me some basics on the computer.
>
> The warmth and joy that embraced us all was decidedly a direct reflection of the attributes that this environment and its teacher seemed to foster. There is no apparent pressure, yet academic and social progress flourishes. I hope to be included next term! Having the opportunity to participate (albeit in a very small way) has been both exciting and a personally uplifting experience.

In my parent volunteer survey, I include a grid asking if or when they might possibly volunteer in the classroom. The grid is blank, only including the times of recess, lunch, specialist times, or when it would be a less appropriate time, and from this I make up a schedule. Every volunteer in the classroom also signs a confidentiality clause, which is kept on file all year long. This is to maintain the privacy of children. Though parents and volunteers can help, the children's levels, interests, or a "bad day" aren't to leave the classroom.

Realistically, no teacher can do everything—especially when there is someone who can read or give the "extra attention" to help develop or reinforce children and specifically, sometimes including those children who you know get no reinforcement at home!

I have some background in music, enough to successfully teach the designated school curriculum. A "master," though, goes above and beyond. One parent had released jazz albums and was known to many for his talent. He never even thought of helping until I called and asked him. The first time he brought his horn and explained music, it became magical. In a genuine openness about his field, the review of notes, scale, and music suddenly came alive. (Even I was drawn in to better appreciate the talent of a musician, along with the love and expression of music.) Many lessons spun off of his presentation. He even returned the next year with his back-up band to play in the multipurpose room for the entire school. Not only a culmination of studies, it encouraged older students who had never thought about it previously to study an instrument. Imagine too, the excitement of the child having dad share his time and talent at school!

From this, other musicians (by hobby) have appeared over the years (guitars, drums, and blues harmonica players). Just as art exudes expression, music is also an art and a release from which some students can grow and benefit. Simple follow-up lessons have directed students to write jingles or poetry and to put thoughts into music. You never know what "talent" might be hiding but I do know what fun learning will/can be.

If you don't have any parents, maybe make some phone calls. In the community, through organizations, find someone to combine your instructional studies with the added dimension of external stimulus. A beautician came in and explained about colors, specifically the color wheel and how colors combine. A former cruise ship singer helped the children to develop specific concepts that they previously had been struggling to memorize by together preparing enticing songs and jingles. A banker discussed money equivalents, savings, the dollar, and from this came studies of international currency, the similarities and differences.

A judge explained the judicial system, the history of our Declaration of Independence and the Constitution. As a result, a mock trial was conducted in the classroom. This took on new interests, studies, readings, organization, preparation and extended in-depth vocabulary. We even had a debate about "causes" throughout history and how outcomes made a difference in our lives today. A grocer came in to discuss advertising, merchandising, and nutrition. I encouraged students to write original advertisements of their own choice. Written enticements and colorful posters were soon created, which evolved into amusing persuasive oral presentations, individually and in peer groups.

A child once asked, "Can I bring my blind uncle for a special lesson?" That was a day of joy because he explained that being blind is just a person with special needs. With his seeing-eye dog, he found his way around the classroom. Open questions children had always wondered about and wanted to ask flowed. Students better understood that all individuals can thrive and such valuable lessons were learned that day! This blind visitor brought with him his Braille typewriter and in front of the children, typed Braille stories while they dictated, as well as typing each of their names.

I met a clown. When asked, he came "normal" into the classroom and told fascinating stories of how it feels to brighten lives and make people smile. He talked of the skills he had studied and acquired, and about being a graduate of clown school. He told of feelings inside a clown gets from going into hospitals to entertain children, as well as being able to bring a moment of highlight to worried parents. We watched a demonstration of clown makeup and the discussion and stories that followed were colorful and deep.

A U.S. military representative fully explained world history as students gathered around a large world map. The United States wars, reasons, leaders, and boundaries were highlighted as well as things never fully explained in my educational studies. A parent who had worked at Renaissance faires came dressed in full attire to make social studies come alive. Our preparation for her arrival included delving into historical accounts of history. We artistically treated paper grocery bags and transformed them into imitation leather and bark, on which students wrote journals and diaries. Readings and discussions developed comparative analogies, which took creative writing lessons to life back then as well as the modern day.

The expression "all in a day's work" is different for everyone —child, student, or adult. Parent involvement, along with significant volunteers, contribute collective and expanded academic mastery to a day at school. For the students, all of these connections are like a trip one takes firsthand.

These experiences stay with them, leaving a lasting impression with an "I did that" feeling. Hopefully, through infinite learning experiences, students will aspire to find their own interests and seek their very own passions.

Mike Wolpert, a dedicated senior volunteer, works weekly by challenging children with specific needs: "Bringing a child that little extra friendship and assistance provides a positive impact in their intellectual growth and well being. My rewards in doing so are the smiles I receive and the inner satisfaction of helping to make a difference."

I remember when I was a child singing a song that "parents are people too." How true that is! I must confess, some of my close personal friends were once parents in my classroom! Our open communication and honesty evolved into what is truly a highlight of my teaching career. Parent involvement has an impact to further our teaching and to help cultivate our students, our children!

I Like Parents So much! thay aRe a big help.

Parents Re good.

Parents help me learn!

Thank you to all who help us.

Parents help us grow.

Parents are Wonderful.

They help me alot

19

LET THEM GIVE TO YOU

I was completely amazed the day I walked into to my classroom and every child was wearing sunglasses! I couldn't help but notice the many unique and different sizes, shapes, colors, and styles!

I had gone out of town for a weekend and a foreign object ended up in my eye. My vision was impaired and the pain was excruciating. I was taken to the hospital where doctors examined and anetheisized my eye. This temporarily alleviated some of the problem, and I received antibiotic eye drops and medication for pain. I was miserable. When I was able to return home on a five-hour flight, I kept moist compresses on my eyes wishing for the pain to subside and for full recovery. When I arrived home, the specialists who treated me told me how fortunate I was because permanent damage often results from severe cornea scratches. I could only resume work if I wore sunglasses. So I did, wondering how that would affect a day's teaching and me personally.

I had guided my student teacher, Laura, into always finding the positives. She sure did! Out of her own money she bought sunglasses for all. Her empathy went beyond as she found a way to make light of what could have been a difficult situation. I will never forget the moment I returned to school. It didn't matter how I looked or how I felt. The class made me feel welcome and was so happy to see me. How many teachers can say they spent a week teaching when everyone wore sunglasses? (And besides that, descriptive stories emerged about all of the wacky, fun, and differ-

Sunglasses for all and a warm welcome.

ent sunglasses.) This student teacher demonstrated the ability to be adaptable and to improvise. She displayed creativity and originality, making good out of an uncomfortable situation. We took quite a group picture, which became a memory for all! This story and that picture were part of Laura's portfolio. She was hired immediately for her first teaching position and she took the power of positive teaching with her!

WHAT A FEELING!

I took students to see a musical production at the Civic Arts Theatre. As the artists on stage played instruments and sang to a full house of 3,000 people, I felt something touch my shoulder. It was my students, on either side of me, who—moved by the songs and experience—had joined arms to sway with the melody. They were reaching out to me! Camaraderie showed they were getting something extra from the concert. I reached out and linked arms, too. This was an unexplainable moment when I felt the harmony and saw the look of satisfaction on their faces. Students were sharing, just because! Students can give indescribable gifts of themselves: their wonderment, unpredictable words, hugs, laughs and excitement, a knowing look, a linger after school, or that special thought or comment.

THEY TAUGHT ME A LESSON!

First-grade student Jeff Butler is now a Berkeley graduate with a degree in electrical engineering. He was a teaching assistant at Berkeley and has a message for all of us:

I learned about what it takes to be a good teacher. I found what worked best was when I put myself in the student's position and thought of all of the questions I would ask. I tried to convey that information first. A teacher who can answer questions is a role model to look up to. It's important for a teacher to be knowledgeable. If I want to master a subject, it makes it much easier if I have a master to follow.

Jeff Butler in first grade.

It's also very important for a teacher to be personable, and to be available outside of class and to encourage students to learn subjects that aren't covered in the classroom. Learning is fun when a concept is presented and is easily followed by application. To apply new knowledge, something must be useful to the student, which requires the teacher to understand what the student thinks is useful. Another trait that helps students learn is constructive criticism. It's perfectly fine for a teacher to tell me that I'm wrong, as long as they tell me what is right so that I can learn from my mistakes. It is more than just telling an answer, it is the time of explanation. Put some fun in the learning process. Explain wrong answers with a joke or an impossible situation that makes students laugh while also realizing why something is the way it is. Building on what you learn is important. I had the most fun when subjects overlapped which helped my retention rate.

Jeff Butler: Berkeley, engineering.

I was taught a lesson for myself personally as well as an educator. To my dismay, I discovered I wasn't as focused or observant as I thought I was. Identical twins were in my class. As I got to know them, I could always tell them apart. Not! I thought I could! One day, just before lunch, my entire class burst out laughing. You see, these twins had switched places that day—their style of dress, hairdo, friends, and even their handwriting. Everyone was in on it, except me! I had taught the class viewing my students on the surface. I was so busy with my lesson, I didn't look into the faces of the twins. It was April Fool's Day and they not only fooled me but also taught me to be more observant.

The next year, I again had these twins. As I drove to school, I thought about what had happened the previous year. No April Fools this time! I wouldn't be fooled again. I was sure of it! I had a great day and the students went to lunch. (This year, their parents planned a trick—they had instructed them not to switch until the afternoon.) They did it again! This generated a multitude of class discussions about awareness, as well as individual characteristics. It tells us as educators our responsibility to be more observant. Don't let your guard down!

A parent of twins shared: "Twins are the same but yet different. One tries desperately to be different, while the other strives to be the same, but yet different." On the subject of twins, everyone has a theory. From my experience, separating them every other year has seemed the healthiest. This way, twins have the chance to develop on their own to grasp self-identity while establishing their own friend relationships. (When together all the time, they often are too connected or speak a twin language.) Twins, like everyone else, want and need to be recognized for their self-identity and who they are!

Every year always has an entirely new challenge! As this book goes to press, I have not one but two sets of twins in my class, and for the first time, triplets! Every student is an individual! Help them cherish their own individuality. What traits or interests separate them from others? Incorporate this philosophy regarding individuality into a discussion of diversity and engage students into helping you list traits on the board. Have students describe their individual characteristics. (As you later review this, they will begin to recognize quality and changes in their character.)

A MYSTERY

There was a loud sound and commotion outside my classroom. Suddenly, thirty-three students walked into class singing a lively tune and each carrying a beautifully, elegantly wrapped gift. (And, oh, those grins! All watching, they couldn't wait to see my reaction.) I was a little (a lot) suspicious, wondering what could this be about. The moment had come when I was overwhelmed. I didn't recall an occasion, but I am the one who teaches there doesn't need to be one. The array of gifts was color-ful, interesting, different, and so unexpected.

My upper-grade students (and parents who joined in on my surprise) continued to sing the lively peanut song they had mastered with volume, hand motions, and pure enthusiasm. On this amazing day, creativity was truly generated back to me. At their insistence, I sat down to open the packages. And so it began. As I opened each of those distinctly wrapped thirty-three gifts, I discovered peanut butter of every size, texture, and label.

Everyone knows my love of peanut butter. I always keep a jar in my cupboard as a protein boost for me or for "starving" students and col-leagues who might also just need a burst of energy. Sometimes we think of the catchy chants the man sings as he throws packages of peanuts to sports fans at Dodger Stadium. Often, I help students make up jingles to achieve retention of a particularly difficult skill or formula. We did taste tests, weight and volume comparisons, descriptive story writing, and multisubject thematic learning. It has been years now, but I can al-most feel the aliveness of that day. They knew me in more ways than one because they more than returned the gift I always try to instill in every child: "Think, enjoy, be creative, and take each thing you study and mas-ter . . . one step further."

ONE PLUS ONE = MORE THAN TWO!

Working one to one can open doors and take a student "beyond." Sitting down with Kendra, she began to write and together we brainstormed. A heartwarming story was the end result. She gave to me the beauty of her thoughts. They were all inside her, just waiting to come out.

A Christmas with Grandma

I am eight years old. I have a story to share that I will tell my children some day when I grow up. I had my first and last Christmas with Grandma. It was a very delightful Christmas and the best one I ever had. I remember two of the presents she got, a fluorescent green gel pen and a small Japanese box. It was a very plain box. I think her sister gave it to her so it was very meaningful and beautiful in Grandma's shining eyes. It was all pencil lead color except for one decorative blue and white triangle down the side of it. The gel pen was from the care lady that helped her. Actually, they became good friends because they both embraced the quality of understanding that they genuinely shared with each other.

Grandma did not give us any material gifts, but she did give us two unforgettable mental presents. Her presence that Christmas and the memory of her that Christmas! My Grandma was able to come down from her room at the end of the hall to the living room where the Christmas tree stood. I wish I had remembered to give her a present. (My teacher says that I did!) She thinks I gave her a most valuable treasure. I spent quality time with Grandma so she wouldn't get lonely. Sometimes I did my homework near her so she could feel my presence. When I came home from school, I would rampage through the house to get to her room. I would bring the gift of my sillies, smiles, and endless abundance of energy. When we watched movies together they became real. Especially if I came in the middle of a movie that she was already watching. You see, she would retell the story with such vigor that I could pretend I had actually seen the beginning.

As I reflect, maybe I did give Grandma something special. I used to bring her breakfast. She said "thank you" to me in a way that I always knew she was very grateful. I can still visualize her smile and that bright twinkle in her eyes. She liked to watch those cooking shows on television. Her favorite was a famous chef who prepared fancy things in only minutes. Though she couldn't eat many of those delicacies, plain toast with green tea was always her dream come true! Sometimes she slept and I was told to just let her be so she could get lots of rest. But when she awakened, my two brothers and I would almost fly to her room to build a fort so we could snuggle just to be near her.

I will never again have the opportunity to give her a real gift, because she died on November 19th the next year, just before Christmas. She was seventy-five years old when she died. Her Japanese name was the same as my middle name, Yukiko, which means snowdrop in Japanese.

On Christmas Eve we have a family dinner with turkey, stuffing, cranberry sauce, green beans, and sparkling cider. I always like the cranberries the best and oh, how Grandma loved the delicious turkey with lots of gravy. Everybody likes gravy! Only my Grandma died the week before Thanksgiving and we all felt sad. Though this time she didn't have the opportunity to share our feast with us, there was far more than sparkling cider at our Thanksgiving table! You see, the memory and sparkle of Grandma filled our holiday and always will in the many years to come.

Now we have planted an herb garden for her. We have really special Japanese peas in there that we just planted. They will grow and grow and we can harvest peas from them. The package says that they are very sweet. I worked hard to plant them with my dad. I helped to prepare the dirt patch. Daddy made the ruts for them and we accomplished all of this together. (She was Daddy's Mommy.) Now everyone that comes to our house will continue to see the progress of the growing peas.

The peas are green. The package says only seventy days for them to grow. There are also red and yellow flowers that we planted across the path in a little garden. I think this Christmas will find the brilliance of the red and yellow flowers blooming along with the peas ready for us on early Christmas morning. In some parts of the world, I just know that this holiday there will be a white Christmas. When I awake in sunny California, I think I will run outside and see the brightness of the holiday just exactly as I know it should be."

THE BEST PRESENT OF ALL

Shhh . . . a "surprise party?" Sometimes the kids really do keep the secret in the excitement of planning one for their teacher, and even if not, each one really is a surprise! One year as I blew out the birthday candles on my cake, a thought came to me about the flickering candles. They were a conglomeration of candles of every color, size, and shape that students had brought from home. They flickered brightly altogether, like my students. As I watched a parent light one candle and use it to light all of the others, it was like when we ignite our students! I noticed that lighting the candles one by one was like reaching my students one by one. Find out your student's special qualities! Know and admire their uniqueness and specialness. One, as individuals, but together, illuminating and beautiful.

STUDENTS GIVE ME SO MUCH

Reading reaches another dimension when children go on a treasure hunt to find facts in newspapers. One day, lying on the floor seeking answers,

Andy said to me, "Ms. Gail, isn't this your ship? The *Fantome*?!" First, I felt such a teacher's joy observing the moment teachers wait for; this "late bloomer" actually reading for content and comprehending. I was so excited! He, with his newly acquired reading skills, proceeded to read to me that the *Fantome* was missing! It took a minute until my comprehension set in. What were his words saying to me? As soon as I could (and it seemed like years), I left the classroom to make the phone call. Oh, the unknown! I didn't know whom to call, so I began by nervously dialing the media. I learned that there was a tropical storm, Hurricane Mitch in the Gulf of Honduras. A four-masted schooner was missing!

I remember the whirling storm in the headlines, news coverage, and endless long days of waiting when the *Fantome* disappeared. The unknown, my sadness, and how I felt inside! Me—who teaches positive— couldn't think of anything positive about this! Children left me little notes and then they asked for an emergency circle. It began with, "We really appreciate you." I wondered what they were saying and I listened, "Ms. Gail, we remember your stories about raising the masts, your memories, exploring, and songs of the sea. We want you to know how happy and positive we all feel!" (Such young children, able to express true empathy with loving sincerity.) I continued to listen, speechless, and feel my emotions. They took turns expressing to me in their own words: "You walked the gangway off of the ship and that is something to be very positive for." "We heard that 18,207 persons died or were lost in that horrible storm." "You will always be able to close your eyes and look at your memories." It was only because of my students that when the news showed pieces of the stairs of the *Fantome* found at sea, I felt a little better. Sad for the loss of a crew of thirty-one that I had just sailed with, happy for my life and for the students who are so much a part of it!

20

9-1-1

Possibilities are endless in teaching, in life! When struggling through a crisis, it is easy to stumble and not look past it. The future at that specific time is yet unknown, but it is the teacher who is responsible for the students, even more so at times of stress. Like a roller coaster, life takes highs, lows, curves, and twists. When these happen, we can't control the racing car going down that bumpy track. We can provide the seatbelt (calmness) to hold the children in during those moments. It is our instincts and attitude that turn the gears and direct the best of a difficult situation.

The Beautiful quilt became a tapestry of Love

Brigette

In a time of catastrophe it is important not only to give direction but also to have materials at your fingertips to engage the children into something other than fear.

Do you have close at hand (within a minute's reach) paper, colored paper, colored pencils, crayons, glue, scissors, accumulated magazines, some paints, a battery-operated musical recorder and soothing musical cassettes (or CDs), indoor "rainy-day" games, nonperishable munchies, gum, water, and a means of staying calm? There are some days that stay with us for a lifetime. When we look back, we wonder how we made it through it all. (Yes, these days happen in teaching too.) They come at a moment when least expected and no one is ever fully prepared for them. When disaster does happen, the way adults react truly affects the children. The above-listed items can actually make a difference in moments of crisis.

Does your school site have emergency plans that all are fully aware of? Is there a backpack near the door to grab in case of evacuation? Suggested contents to include: flashlight, radio, batteries, thermal blankets, notes from parents if younger children are involved, and current parental release forms.

Once, at a nearby school district, a fire swept through the canyon. Emergency procedures were thoroughly executed within minutes, including buses that arrived and carried hundreds of student and staff members to safety. When all sighed with relief at the successful evacuation and secure feeling, there was one glitch. Several emergency forms were incomplete or not current and students could not be released to friends, neighbors, or caring individuals. Because of this, I encourage schools to find a way to check emergency releases so that they are maintained, updated, and thorough (maybe—simply because you are prepared —they will never even be needed).

Learning takes place in all that a child encounters, in their questions, curiosities, and the many things that they see, hear, and experience. As I think about it, every "event" affects the children!

JANUARY 1986

Our TVs were specially connected to watch the launch of the *Challenger*. It was the first time an astronaut/teacher was not only selected, but was going to present a lesson to America's schoolchildren from outer space. Planet mobiles and space shuttle replicas dangled in my classroom. Science lessons, which had been geared towards space exploration, had been successfully mastered. A true day in American history! Everyone was dressed in red, white, and blue as discussion flowed everywhere throughout an entire country about going to space. In unison, America shared the curiosity, wonderment, pride, and accomplishments in modern science about to transpire before our very eyes.

"Ten . . . nine . . . eight . . . seven . . ." Young children, all children, teens, and adults had practiced for the countdown. Our country's successful space exploration was significant for the future of rockets, space missions, and science. History was being made and suddenly, Americans shared the unexpected silence within one minute after liftoff as the spaceship disintegrated due to a leak in the booster rockets' fuel lines, and was gone.

Unexplainable! Unexpected . . . and children wanted many answers. I was numb. We took a moment of silence. The kids, on their own, began to draw magnificent pictures. It was a natural response and we filled the walls with their expressive artwork. We talked about feelings, sadness, and how the entire world would learn from what went wrong. A strong international connection of sorrow resulted from such a tragedy.

I involved my students in cutting red, white, and blue streamers that became part of the classroom décor, helping them to ease their unexplained feelings. We were creating, our country faced a loss, and yet we still needed to forge forward—for the tomorrows.

FROG MAN IN WET SUIT . . . ON THE ROOF

Years ago, I was in the staff room sharing hearty laughter with colleagues and in one second, the lightness of that day changed. Law enforcement officers entered our lounge demanding that we literally drop everything and go at once into the adjoining school cafeteria. Those children who had been playing freely on the playground quickly joined the children eating in the cafeteria. Five hundred children emerged together, all wondering what was this special occasion. (The only thing our staff had been told was "danger, man in wetsuit reported on school roof with weapons.") I can still picture one astute little first-grade boy as he looked to me in fear saying, "We don't usually do this type of thing and something is wrong!"

Hundreds of children were confined to the school cafeteria indefinitely. I remember the loud sounds of police helicopters, the sight of trained canines, and numerous officers risking their safety for our children. I recall the sounds as some children whined and others began to cry. As time went on (which seemed like forever), most of the children (ages five through twelve) realized (though we strived to keep them calm) that something was wrong. They couldn't play freely, and could not go to the bathrooms or outside. It is situations like this when the guidance of a teacher is more meaningful than ever. Though we cannot guarantee "safety," we can do everything we can to keep them as safe as possible. This is beyond any textbook training, it is common sense.

A colleague and I clapped our hands for the children to fall into an echoing response. Before anyone realized it, they were absorbed in what we were doing. Time began to pass as children joined us in silly songs, attempted rounds, and hand motions.

Though the "frogman in wetsuit" scrambled over rooftops and somehow got away, five hundred children made it through the day. Through police escorts (including the fascinating canine team), school was dismissed and students were released for the day. Though they never caught the man who threatened an entire school, somehow we all caught the taste of unity!

FIREMEN AT SCHOOL!

Firemen fascinate many young children—their bright yellow trench coats, those big tall black boots, loud sirens, and the storybook memories about firemen sliding quickly down ladders. One day, unexpected firemen rushed into my classroom as well as all of the classrooms throughout the entire school. This was not a visit, however, nor the culmination of a social studies unit. It was reality.

The Malibu fire, only a few miles away, had begun and was out of control. Because of possible smoke inhalation, though we were not in immediate danger of the fire, everyone in the school was ordered to stay inside the classrooms. We got out paint and made freeform designs. Children named their creative masterpieces. Some made them into cards and others wrote descriptive stories about their paintings. Hours later, school closed early and children were released to parents and those on their emergency forms.

I remember the day following and the long days of a fire that raged out of control. Firemen were brought in from out of state to contain and control the destructive Malibu fire that changed areas almost like a chess game. Though we were safe at school, our focus on regular lessons was obviously not the same as usual. My students and I squeezed fresh locally grown lemons and made lemonade. We measured the ingredients for varied cookie recipes and we took the results to the local park where firemen were temporarily living as they rotated shifts. I heard a fireman on a phone to loved ones describing the fire and that he was somewhere, he didn't know exactly where, called Newbury Park.

How happy we were to share our homemade lemonade and cookies with the dirty faced and tired firemen, in return for those smiles that we received. The children saw frightened horses being led to safety and viewed firsthand the dedication that rescue workers, including volunteers, give to save lives and cities. Being positive is something that continuously helps those who are lucky enough to have this valuable trait, as well as the ability to extend and share it with others!

LOCKDOWN

Just a regular day! (Not that any day in teaching is ever "regular.") "Lockdown," we were told over a speaker, "No one has permission to go outside." Now this was something new and different. Bank robbers were loose within the vicinity and precaution was being taken so they wouldn't come to hide in the school or take any hostages.

Doors were locked and windows, too. "Don't go near the windows and no one can leave the room," I heard myself saying. Once they realized this was not a game, tears and fears flowed (especially one little girl

I did not even know, who had merely come to visit because she was soon to be in my class).

Hmmmm . . . I thought to myself as the loud hum of police helicopters roared overhead. I knew I was the "role model" and calmness needed to prevail; it is truly up to the teacher to initiate staying calm and to make light of the situation. So we sat together quietly as I read some favorite stories and, though they knew I was stalling, we entered into discussion about the stories. Time passed and so did the disaster. Luckily, our school was spared further problems than just that of a lockdown, though all appreciated the precautionary measures. Sadly, a woman was killed and the robbers were never found. Years have passed, yet some of us wonder and remember when we hear and see helicopters overhead.

EMERGENCY SITUATIONS

Some might necessitate silence and no movement—blinds closed and hope of no one entering a secure, locked classroom. Though at times it has truly ached inside in my stomach (from fear, unknown, and worry), it is my outside that the children see and need to gain the safe feelings.

When it has been an emergency that does not have to remain silent, I have told children to just pretend it is a "rainy day." "Snow day?" (This can apply to students of any age.) Unstructured drawing, art, free reading, favorite music, fun, and how about silly games like marbles and Twister?

When an unexpected negative occurrence happens, find a way to channel their energy into something positive. Occupy their time in any emergency or unusual situation, and it is possible they won't even want it to end!

SEPTEMBER I I, 2001

Some children heard about it when they woke up, or on the way to school, and some had no idea. We were told not to discuss it at school, yet my instincts told me that it would have to be addressed in some manner. People in New York were trying to find their loved ones. Parents and teachers throughout the entire world were attempting to find some small way to assure their children. No one wants any child, anywhere, to go to sleep at night with sadness or fear. Emotions flowed as we all grasped for thoughts about the tragedy.

I told my students, "You will always remember this day. Like me, I remember the day that President Kennedy was shot." I asked them to appreciate the safe feeling knowing that we have each other to be with, in good times and bad.

My students drew random pictures on September 11th and placed them together on the floor. It was inspiring that they could release the unknown inside them through the beauty of art. The configuration of their drawings assembled on the floor appeared to me like a tapestry of the inner workings of children.

The quilt.

From this, came the idea of a quilt, which has added dimension and enrichment to many lives. The making of our quilt was a project started to channel my kids' energy into a positive learning experience. Students brought old clothes and scraps of material to school. Cutting and sewing lessons began. They learned how to thread a needle, tie a knot, and sew a seam. Joining in this project were 120 children from Open Classroom, ages five through twelve, who truly learned how to

collaborate. Piece by piece, stitch by stitch, their fingers created a masterpiece beyond my expectations.

Instead of dwelling, we were doing—and learning actually thrived because a cohesive group of children were working together. Children wrote poetry and heartfelt stories, finding descriptive words to heighten the skills of written language. Every individual felt tremendous satisfaction participating in many forms of self-expression.

As time went by, the idea came to me of combining this learning experience with a humanitarian gesture. One young child said it all, "Everyone needs something to be thankful for." For Thanksgiving, we sent our writings and the quilt to the school that faced the Twin Towers in New York, where students had watched the horrible event and lost family members. We gave them something to be thankful for on Thanksgiving and every day thereafter. Our poetry, writings, and giant quilt are displayed in New York for all to share and students in California feel the impact of collectively reaching out to others.

From this negative, we created a positive. We turned sadness into joy. I would like to share with you relevant comments surrounding that unforgettable day of September 11th.

From Brenda Yoshinaga, a parent:

I will never forget what I heard at 8:02 when I turned on the radio that day. Manhattan shrouded in smoke?? What is going on? My blood ran cold; who was this enemy? When I arrived at school, Gail and her students were quietly sitting in circle, discussing feelings and fears.

When I took my children home and discussed that the United States had been attacked, with probably thousands of people killed, their eyes grew big, and they silently tried to make sense of it. When we got home, I told my bedridden mother-in-law. The tears streamed down her face; she vividly remembered Pearl Harbor, and as a Japanese-American, saw her father being taken away at bayonet point to an internment camp. My family now didn't want to be apart from each other.

The idea of the quilt I thought was a brilliant idea, to comfort these kids suffering through such a terrible time. Parents helped the children bring in fabric and lent their expertise, teaching the kids how to sew and blend the squares together. It took weeks to complete and we were all very excited when the quilt was shipped to New York. Gail shared e-mails from the school in New York where it was displayed. They were overwhelmed and the quilt became an American symbol of comfort, remembrance, and care. Through the quilt, students, parents, and teachers shared feelings with their counterparts in New York.

An e-mail from New York:

Wow!! My students went wild. We had no idea your kids were making a real quilt. They kept running into the hall to see it! The quilt is fantastic!

I understand now why you did not want to let it go. We are deciding on the best place to put it up. We want it to be in an area where there is a lot of student traffic and where it can stand out alone. We will send you photos of this. Some of our students are writing your kids thank you letters.

You did a masterful job organizing and teaching your students this wonderful skill. They have sewed a masterpiece! Every one of us is touched by this work and art of love. The girl who lost two family members had to get her emotions in order. The care given by California students really hit her Monday. I was deeply moved myself. Thanks again for making our students smile and allowing them this emotional release.

Counselor LuNel LeMieux says:

It was my delight to be able to view a remarkable quilt created by children. In this world where many seem to be scurrying about, it was very touching to know that children took the time to say how much they cared about others they did not even know but could in their own way feel the pain and fear experienced in New York. The students put a great amount of love and thought into each stitch. This is compassion, empathy, and healing at its best—being active and doing something that will make a difference for a very long time.

Caring kids are a wonderful example to all of us and they may be the ones leading the way to creating a better world. I hope this selfless expression of reaching out to their "brothers and sisters" will be spotlighted and serve as a torchlight for all of us to remember how it is supposed to be. (LeMieux 2002)

Words of visitor Randi Dubin King:

It was my honor and privilege to view the quilt that students made for the children in New York. I was amazed by their ability to identify and empathize with others. Their initiative and creativity is remarkable. Such an incredibly challenging project is to be admired. I had the opportunity to talk with the kids about their participation in the quilt, and I was touched at how proud and honored they felt to be a part of this special, heartfelt project. They each chose special pieces of meaningful cloth to include in their individual patches for the quilt. They were very moved and concerned for the children who had witnessed such a horrific tragedy.

The children worked cooperatively together and I was very impressed at their ability to speak so openly about their own thoughts and feelings. Their strong sense of self allows them to feel secure within their own community. This is a perfect example of how to make a difference in the lives of others.

Debbie Bavarro, a parent, says:

When they decided to make the quilt, it was like therapy. When they decided to send the quilt, it was empowering. Not just for children, but for everyone involved. The project took on a new feel, warmer and more intense.

When pictures from New York came to us, it was like finishing the jig-saw puzzle, that last piece in place. The children were very proud and happy to hear what a wonderful response their quilt had inspired. I only hope that the children in New York can appreciate how much they really gave back, by accepting the gift and by validating the honest and heartfelt caring of the children here.

Robert H. Sinclair, the principal in New York, expressed these closing thought in June: "The staff and students of Science Skills Center wish to thank the students of Thousand Oaks, California, for their sensitivity and carefully executed work in the beautiful quilt, which is displayed in our lobby. . . . 'In times of danger and travail, we know that goodness will prevail'" (Sinclair 2002)

Also included with his words were these poems from students in New York:

"I Celebrate Myself"

I Celebrate Myself
The life I share, we share
The breath I breathe, we breathe
The things I celebrate (the sun, life)
You should celebrate
This is the world we live in:
I celebrate my sense of humor
I celebrate my ability to eat a lot.
I celebrate my great ability to withhold the pain
Sent by the World.

——by John Addison

I Celebrate Myself by
Smiling. Once I smile everybody's
Heart opens up to me. My smile
Is just another way to show
That everything gonna be okay.
Once somebody see me smile,
There's no more rainy days for them.
My smile is just another
Way to tell everybody they special.
I celebrate myself by smiling

——by Nickflor Jean

"I Celebrate Myself"
I celebrate myself when I'm happy
I do when I'm say**
Although it may not be the best time
But it makes me feel glad.
I celebrate myself when I think
I do when I cry
Although it may not be the best time
But it makes me smile
Year we become strong,
We all have our good days and bad
Having nightmares makes you scream.
But, know you for many years brings
Back memories.
Now, that's what you can a good dream.
We thank God for you and many others.
It's hard to find words for you.
But these are very easy. . . . And they
Are: Thank You!
We know you really care.
Thank you for being there.***
You've always said school's a must, ***
Thank you for showing your trust,
Life sometimes go sour like lemons and
Limes. Thanks for having time.

Friendship reminds me of a dove.
But most of all,
Thank you for showing your love!

—Janie Uddin

"Thanks, We Love You"—Robert Sinclair, principal

Our outlook as educators influences all of those whom we teach. It is my hope that disasters are all behind us. Realistically, though, parents and educators must always be prepared and "be there" in times of need. Our students, who are the future, articulate and express their hopes and dreams for world peace.

"World Peace," by Sky McLeod (age 8),
First Place, National Poetry Contest

Peace is the strongest thing on earth
But can't even pick up a crumb
It's impossible for peace to be spread around the world
Like bread and butter
Good couldn't be judged
Good would turn boring.
Boring isn't peace,
Peace isn't boring.
Peace is like water
On a drizzling day
But sometimes
You wish it was pouring

Sky McLeod: poet.

"How I Remember," by Kendra Yoshinaga (age 7)
Ventura County Poetry Winner

One early September morning
As I went to school
I had no idea
That this very morning
Would be an instant source
Of hatred and sadness for all of America.
I came into the room
To find complete mayhem—
I thought there had been a fire
In a few minutes I learned
Of the terrible bombing of
New York, and the Pentagon.
Mommy came in crying
And we went home.
Early in the morning.
Little had I known
This would become a day
I would never forget.

"The Power of Peace" by Micaela Bavaro (age 8)

Peace is the sun that rises in the early morning,
Peace is the wind in the willows,
Peace is the ambers in a fire,
Peace is everywhere! Can you feel it?

A QUILT MADE WITH LOTS OF LOVE IN EACH AND EVERY STITCH

WE HOPE TO BRIGHTEN YOUR DAYS WITH EXTRA HAPPINESS AND COLOR ~ ~ ~ ~

YOU ARE IN OUR THOUGHTS---ALWAYS!!!!

XOXOXOXOXOXOXOXOXOXOXOXOXOO

Students expressed their feelings:

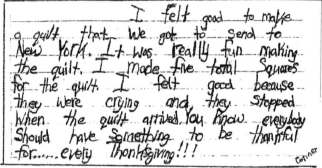

I felt good to make a quilt that we got to send to New York. It was really fun making the quilt. I made five total squares for the quilt. I felt good because they were crying and they stopped when the quilt arrived. You know everybody should have something to be thankful for.....every Thanksgiving!!!

Conner

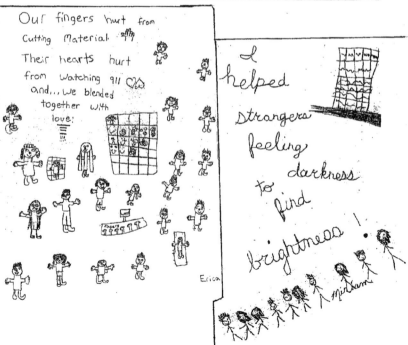

Our fingers hurt from cutting material. Their hearts hurt from watching 911 and,,,we blended together with love.

Erica

I helped strangers feeling darkness to find brightness!

Miriam

AND IN CONCLUSION
COMES ONLY A BEGINNING

Dear Jake-I hoqe
you are not sard
becos I can not wate
Tel you cum back.

In this day and age when test scores are so highly stressed, I still feel that human experiences touching human lives will raise the test scores. If a child has confidence, he or she can walk into the test situation, sit down, and begin perhaps ten points ahead. When children feel good deep inside, every step of their educational development will be self-empowering.

My senses were heightened as I heard the tick tock of the clock on the wall and watched the black hands slowly go around, minute by minute and hour by hour. Sitting in the hospital waiting room while someone special is in surgery is a restless and draining experience (especially when it is an elected surgery, brought on by me!).

At the onset, I felt exuberance, but that little red second hand became almost too much to watch. My heart was pounding as I began to feel queasy and scared. The hours continued to pass with no word. I looked to my right to see Mom, Auntie, and Sister almost green with worry, and to my left was Grandma's face, which was more than self-explanatory. All of us were wondering the same thing: should we even be there at all?

Thoughts began to run rampant through my head, about me. (Maybe I do too much in my teaching? Is this a lesson?) Until these moments, I truly had followed my philosophy that there is always that little something a teacher can do to reach each child and make the difference. Lost in thought, I was startled to see the doctor appear in front of me. As I watched him take off his mask I knew this was the moment and suddenly I could see a genuine smile from ear to ear. That sight of the man in green gave me more than relief, it confirmed my dedication as an educator. You see, the patient who had finally come through long hours of surgery and who was now in recovery was my student!

Jake came to me without self-esteem. His mother changed his school because where he came from peers harassed him and he cried every night. Can you imagine going through life with a distorted face? A young child exposed to the cruelty of people's stares and insensitive comments, he carried a burden. This burden molded Jake's negative self-esteem.

I vividly remember the day Jake first appeared at my door. He was teary eyed, self-conscious, and afraid of another rejection. By mid-morning, the children called for an "emergency circle" to include him in our family. It was all Jake could do to sit still, but I know he was listening. Friendly chatter transpired as children shared that they were glad he came to our class. We almost needed another circle after recess. My cuties were almost fighting just to be with Jake on the playground. He certainly wasn't alone anymore! By the end of the first day, everyone already knew that this new boy, Jake, was a great athlete. I teach my students to look, feel, and find the positives. My kids accepted Jake from the inside out. As days went by, we came to realize that Jake had a silly sense of humor that could make anyone smile.

Just as thematic teaching includes multisubjects to take students beyond the everyday curriculum, the story of Jake is thematic, too. Our coursework became related with Jake's plight. I clearly remember the first school picture day when he not only became out of control, but he went and hid because there was no way he would allow any one to take his photograph! This boy who was a major behavior problem and who had been acting out because of his lack of self-esteem was now giving so much to me and my students!

He opened our eyes to what handicapped people experience. Imagine the circles when we sat and listened to Jake's stories, which seemed so unbelievable yet were true. My students in that class not only accepted Jake but they tried to understand the words he so openly expressed. In class discussions, the children sounded so mature, almost as if they each had lived the handicap of being different.

Eventually, he too was smiling. Gradually, he opened up in circle. He shared how it felt to go to the market and have total strangers say thoughtless things to him. There was such silence in my room as we all used our listening skills and learned lessons far beyond any textbooks. Compassion surfaced and those students learned lessons they will take with them throughout their entire lifetime. This experience, I know, will make each of us a better human being and more appreciative of who we are.

It is those little things that snowball into the most special moments. The day before Jake went to the hospital, our circle was astounding and is recorded in my memory forever. Children were asking, "But why do you have to have this surgery anyway?" "We like you just the way you are." Children were now worrying that Jake might be different and not the same Jake when he returned. This is an example of how communication benefits the learning environment.

As you begin to feel the benefits of having communicative interaction in your classroom, you will understand that there will be times that you know you couldn't have scripted anything better. Your students can take you to higher dimensions by the things they say and the questions they ask. Being able to communicate is empowering! It enables us to share our hopes, dreams, fears, and feelings. It fosters positive self-esteem. When you release what is inside of you, and are accepted by your teacher and peers, the whole world opens up to you. Suddenly, all those negative feelings are washed away and there is time for more focus and concentration. Your students will also take on more ownership in their classroom and will interact more effectively with people. New doors in family relationships will open as children grasp the vital skills of verbal expression.

Empathy appeared in the daily writings of my students. When children are guided to continuously write their thoughts, the written language begins to flow in all academic areas. Students can better express themselves. The skills of written language will expand because developing the "whole child" entails not only confidence and self-esteem, but also the ability to share in every possible way.

As you have learned in previous chapters, when challenging activities and aliveness in their learning environment turn on students, they will be more motivated in all academic endeavors. When students are highly motivated, they become like sponges ready to soak up as much as you give them.

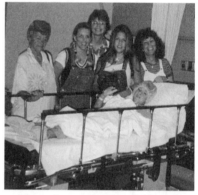

As I drove to the hospital in that early morning darkness, the profound impact of what was about to happen was suddenly overwhelming to me. There were so many thoughts that ran through my head. Jake had been transformed from the inside out and was now about to be transformed from the outside in.

Jake on the gurney, surrounded by family members (me on the right) and ready to be wheeled into surgery (under the pillow is the folder of inspirational letters from friends and classmates).

I had made a choice to do something I truly believed in, to help another human being. Taking off a day of work to be there with my student and his family during surgery was beyond the teachers editions and core curriculum guides. I was going there not for myself, but for a child. Isn't that what teaching is all about? I learned from this, though, not to let the little things get you down. Maybe that is what the expression "out of the box" truly means—being there and always finding ways to reach the students! Go forward with

The new life begins! Thumbs up, as Jake begins to recover in style and with excited curiosity as to what he will look like.

what you believe in and extend a positive attitude to the children. The rewards are beyond any math calculations you will ever do, for they are countless.

It was late in the day when I made that phone call. I called the school and they transferred the call to the classroom. With tears flowing, I shared that Jake was out of surgery and in the recovery room. I told them how he loved their special stories and letters, which were in a yellow folder that had actually gone with him on the gurney into surgery. As it was announced over the speaker to the classroom, I could hear the loud screams and cheers of celebration (and I know the substitute in my classroom that day must have understood).

These moments have added depth and unity to my students and to me as a person. Teaching has given me so much and continues to do so each and every day. The day of surgery was a bright one after all, just like my favorite color of yellow! Brightness is something different to each and every unique and special human being. As you close this book, it is my hope that you will open yourself to add a little extra pizzazz to your every tomorrow.

We are all alike and different—that is a theme that can stretch in every direction. Chart it, graph it, write about it, talk about it, and know that is the secret of a special teacher. It is the sensitivity and encouragement one gives to children while guiding them to be responsible for their own behaviors. What a better world this would be if each of us gave children the gift of skills necessary to overcome personal challenges that might interfere during the span of being a child and into adulthood.

Buy a package of animal crackers and ask the students to sort them. How many ways can they sort them? One way is to record the attributes that are the same and different—type of animal/size/location/markings. Challenge the students to write about this in a story, poetry, or illustration, depending on age. Conduct a class meeting to study and discuss each other's findings from their animal box. And then, how many in all? Elephants? Rhinos? Unicorns? Can you write a script or puppet show about people and their special needs? Write a play or a song and find compatible literature too. Write about it!

I believe in the education and success of the "whole child." The significance of my writing this book is to share a myriad of proven techniques. It is my intention that each of these chapters will help educators and

parents to encourage and assist children in being
the best they can be.

Jake's mom is now a preschool teacher. She
teaches with extra sparkle and her burst of sun-
shine reaches young children with extra depth
and warmth. Recently, I went to dinner with
Jake, his extended family, and Barbara Romey.
(After many coincidences, she was the contact
that helped to make this all possible by intro-
ducing us to a world-renowned facial recon-
structive surgeon, Dr. George Orloff.) At the
restaurant, we all sat in a quiet corner.

Jake begins junior high.

Jake smiled his beautiful radiant smile (the
same one we saw, even before surgery). We
were not quiet for long when the family told
the story of how I had called one night asking,
"Do you mind if I ask a personal question?"
The question had merely been, "If I could get
help for your child, would you be in agreement?" This brought an abundance of laughter
and flowing tears as Jake's family was bursting
to tell the story of how the phone chain began
that one night years ago. They imitated each

Jake growing up.

other answering their telephones and the dis-
cussions that followed throughout that night and still continue. ("Was
this teacher crazy, what could she possibly do for us?") As educators, I
hope my readers will remember my message: we can *always* do a little
something for our students.

I invite you now to look at comments by and involving Jake. At the
holiday show that first December, Jake tried to sing. At the holiday show
one year later, Jake stood in the front row, center, sang with glee, and co-
incidentally it was his picture that appeared in two different newspapers. Not because I told anyone, but because he was the child who stood
out, beaming and singing with vigor. He had become a whole child!

Every day

is always the best. . . .

and

even . . . a ~~bad day~~

can

be turned around into

something positive.

Turn the page upside down to see for yourself!!!!

Excerpts of writings from young classmates, new friends, first week of school~

Dear Ms. Gail, I'm sad for Jake. Your a swell teacher. I love you.

I em sad that Jake has to stay home.

I wud fele nrvis to if I was gone to a I nere had a Obrashun. dot no how you feel. hosple.

Jake is going in the oparashan toom. I feel sory for him.

Jake are you happy. I'm happy for you. god Jake.

Daer Ms. gail Jake is very brave. Ms. gail is going to be there. They are going to fix his nose. Jake is scared but happy

Excerpts from Jake's daily writing....Pre-surgery~

Dear Journal I'm going too have a surgary on my nose. I'm not excited or glad i'm really, really Scared!

Jake

That is normal to be SCARED. I am sooo excited and happy for you Jake!!! Please write me more ~♡ ms. Gail ☺

Dear miss Gail- I don't think I wonna get this sugary done. Im like really scared and kind of excited.

Jake

Your and thoughts and feelings are O.K. You are the best Jake!!!

I've lost friends soooo many times and I hert more times and I will propaly be gail how come it has to be so complacatid? I wish I could get them all back!

Jake- I know mean... what you don't know... I the answers... You are an important person in my life. ☺ ms. Gail ☺

REFERENCES

Benjamin, Arthur. 2002. Mathemagician, professor, Harvey Mudd College.

Delisle, Jim. 2002. Professor, Kent State University.

Glasser, William. 1969. *Schools without Failure*. New York: Harper and Row.

———. 1999. *Choice Theory*. New York: Harper Collins.

———. 2000. *Every Student Can Succeed*. Chula Vista, Calif.: Black Forest Press.

Hill, John. *A Child Works in the Sunlight Hoping for a Chance*, 11.

Holliman, Connie. 2002. *A Classroom of Unique Behavior Cars*, Reality Therapy.

Hultgren, Del. 2002. Speech and language specialist, Char-del Communications.

LeMieux, LuNel. Maple Counseling Center staff, tribes trainer, UCLA Center for Human Development, Reality Therapy.

Liewen, Antoinette C. Retired Los Angeles Superior Court Commissioner.

McIntosh, Helen. www.peacerug.com, certified in Glasser Reality Therapy, 1999.

Morgan, Shante. 2003. Journalist, professor of Journalism/Communications, California Lutheran University.

Nelson-Odbäck, Åsa. 1997. *Pocket Coach to Parenthood*. (Santa Barbara, Calif.: Light Beams Press).

O'Grady, Christy. 2001. www.reptilefamily.com.

Phillips, Debora. 1989. *How to Give Your Child a Great Self-Image*. New York: Plume.

Sinclair, Robert H., principal of Science Skills Center-New York.

Vestuto, Rhoda. 2001. Speech pathologist, children's author.

ABOUT THE AUTHOR

Gail Small has her master's degree in education and has taught in the Conejo Valley of southern California for thirty-three years. She has taught many age levels, which have included gifted, troubled, high-risk, learning-disabled, bilingual, main-streamed, and multi-aged students. Her experience in-cludes working with Glasser Quality School Consortium, IDEA League of Innovative Schools, Early Childhood Education Model School, Madelyn Hunter Clinical Teaching Demon-stration School, the Gifted Children's Association staff, Open Class-room, International student tour director, and delegation leader for People to People Student Ambassador Program. She has been a master teacher and consulted with teacher training programs at Pepperdine University, California State Universities, California Lutheran University, and Moorpark College. Named to *Who's Who in American Colleges and Universities*, she is a student advocate who wants to make a difference by reaching educators everywhere.

Ms. Small brings to life the one-on-one relationship with each student. She is a motivational speaker who has spoken at universities and international educational conferences, was named a Fulbright Memorial Scholar, and was an ambassador to Japan. While in Japan, she spoke on her favorite topic: self-esteem. Her love of travel has taken her throughout the world and she incorporates this into thematic teaching and motivational themes.